Living in the Anointing

Steps in Discipleship
Empowered by the Spirit

Juan José Churruarín

Sovereign World

Sovereign World Ltd
PO Box 777
Tonbridge
Kent TN11 0ZS
England

Original title: *El Precio de la Uncion*
Translated from Spanish by John Plumb
Originally published as *The Cost of the Anointing*.
Copyright © 1995 Juan José Churruarín

ISBN: 1 85240 276 8

This Sovereign World book is distributed in North America by
Renew Books, a ministry of Gospel Light, Ventura, California,
USA. For a free catalog of resources from Renew Books/
Gospel Light, please contact your Christian supplier or
call 1-800-4-GOSPEL.

Typeset by CRB Associates, Reepham, Norfolk
Printed in England by Clays Ltd, St Ives plc.

Dedication

This work is dedicated to the people of God. It is my desire to inspire the reader to live a life deeper in the dimension of the Spirit. Despite the revival that the church has been experiencing over recent years, there is still a large sector of Christians who remain indifferent and who have conformed to a lower standard of life than that which was purposed by God. At this historic time in God's dealings with humanity there is an urgent need to know what must now be done. If we do not develop God's plan we shall not only be in default of his requirements but we will have let down this generation and the next. Our inheritance has been gained by effort and sacrifice. At the start it was written with the blood of Jesus, and our forefathers over many centuries continued to write it with their lives. What will we do for the Lord and for his Cause? These pages are written for you with all my heart.

J.J. Churruarín

Acknowledgements

Our new birth in Christ was brought about by a person who was chosen by God and used to bring us to the knowledge of the truth. The lives of many others have contributed in our walk with the Lord and continue to do so, supporting us with their ministry until we all reach fullness in Christ. If I had to mention all those who have edified me, I would run the risk of omitting some of them. I give thanks to the Lord for the consecrated lives and efforts of these men, many of whom are my personal friends. Their lives have presented to me a godly challenge and they continue to be a living witness of love, faith and sacrifice. Some of them are like a holocaust, a sacrifice which is being consumed as a whole burnt offering in the greatest cause that man has ever known: **Jesus**, our great passion.

Hundreds of men and women pray and fast on my behalf. I am indebted to them in the Lord. I am, together with my family, the product of the Love of God and the love of the Great Family of God. To all, my sincere thanks.

Contents

Introduction

*'He has delivered us from the power of darkness and
conveyed us into the kingdom of the Son of His love.'*
(Colossians 1:13 NKJV)

Our nature was changed when we were transferred into
this kingdom. We have been born of God by his own will
and consent. We were literally created anew by the operation of the Holy Spirit. We have been given a new life.

Our first experience of salvation is not of factual knowledge, rather of an encounter with Jesus. We were slaves
and he set us free. This is the greatest miracle that we
have received; when our whole being was set on fire by
the flame of first love. During our first steps we just
observed God's great demonstrations of his power in
answer to our needs. Like the people who came out of
slavery in Egypt; they saw great signs and miracles. Like
the first followers of Jesus; they were witnesses of the
great works of the Lord. The primitive church also came
to life with great demonstrations of the power of God.
However, there comes a time to take on responsibility.
The people who came out of Egypt had to face the desert.
The disciples, a handful of virtually defenceless men,
watched their Lord and Master hang on a cross; and the
newly born church had to face persecution. It is at this

point that we begin what I call 'the process', which intensifies *like the first gleam of dawn, shining ever brighter till the full light of day* (Proverbs 4:18). The Word of God calls it 'walking in Christ' (Colossians 2:6 KJV). It consists not of leaps but of steps. There are no short-cuts, no shortening of the road, no cutting out stages. It is a steady formation of the character of Jesus in our lives through a series of small goals at successive levels of spiritual growth. God's great desire is to have a family of children all like the Lord (Romans 8:29). Thus we need to reach the whole measure of the fullness of Christ. This is not the work of men, for,

> *'He who began a good work in you will carry it on to completion until the day of Christ Jesus.'*
>
> (Philippians 1:6)

For this work God instituted some to be apostles, some to be prophets, some to be evangelists, and some to be pastors and teachers, until we reach unity in the faith and the whole measure of the fullness.

We could never do it alone. Father God has made it so that we can only grow with the mutual help of the other members of the Body of Christ. In unity and one accord, through the activity of each member, we will grow and build ourselves up in love (Ephesians 4:11–16).

No-one can be prepared, much less perfected, if they have not been born into the new dimension of the Kingdom of God. People may be a 'congregation' without being a 'body'. We may apply new methods and techniques, we may erect the scaffolding, but that is not the building.

God has his way of doing things, and nobody can be built up without first entering into the flow of God's Spirit. This is the only way to discover the **anointing** for service.

Chapter 1

The Call

'For God's gifts and his call are irrevocable.'
(Romans 11:29)

God chose us in Christ before the creation of the world, to be 'holy and blameless in his sight'. In love he predestined us to be 'adopted as his sons through Jesus Christ', in accordance with his pleasure and will – to the praise of his glorious grace, which he has freely given us in the One he loves. 'We did not choose him but he chose us'. And 'he appointed us to go and bear much fruit' – fruit that will last.

This truth is enough to overwhelm us. We could never before have imagined it. To think..., that we were predestined by God to be his adopted sons through Jesus Christ! Now we know that the curtain in the temple was not torn from bottom to top. Man did not reach God, but God reached man. God extended the bridge to us. Man could not make himself equal to God, so God took on human likeness so that we could become like him. We were chosen to express his glory. All we do in our experience of God's purposes is to discover what he prepared in advance for us to do. We were born to know him, in order to taste his great love and mercy. On reading about the early history of man, the uninformed could get the wrong impression that God had failed. The woman was deceived and consequently, with his eyes open, Adam also sinned. Just as the fall began with a woman, God began the Great Salvation giving us his Son, born of a woman. The same wedge of weakness used by Satan to ruin humanity was used by Father God to give us his only Son, and with him the revelation of the hidden mystery of the ages, turning it into an instrument of blessing.

Even angels long to look into these things, but are not permitted. The church is spectacular both in the natural and the spiritual world. The spiritual forces of evil take note when the people of God advance, releasing on their way the glorious resources of the divine economy. Long ago the prophets, men most sensitive to God, sought intently to know at what time these things would be fulfilled. They were amazed, captivated by what would take place; the King of the heavens made man. 'Emmanuel' – 'God with us' – tortured and killed because of our rebellion; raised in power and glory. Death, hell and the devil defeated for ever. The promise of the Father, the Holy Spirit, poured out upon the whole of humanity, never imagined before. Free access to God through the new and living Way; our Lord Jesus Christ, and his Church, the new community that would change the course of history with eternal and momentous repercussions.

God in his manifold wisdom could have chosen other means to carry through his redemptive purpose. But no, he wanted to achieve man's salvation by means of a man. Let us understand that though the jar without treasure is just a jar of clay, there could be no treasure without the jar to contain it; to show that this all-surpassing power is from God and not from us.

This planet was shaken by divine judgment long before man was created; and once created the earth was again shaken by another universal judgment in the days of Noah. In view of this the God-created beings, the heavenly armies who inhabit a different sphere from ours, would be looking expectantly for the events that would follow. They were the first to be astonished and give glory and an uncontainable torrent of praise to the Highest when the tender cry of that gentle and sweet baby boy was first heard. All of creation, which had been subjected to a curse because of man, applauded rejoicing in him. Moreover the foundations of hell itself trembled, and Lucifer with them. From then on Satan began to lose, until he was totally overthrown by Jesus on the cross. God wanted to show in the centuries to come his kindness towards us and the abundant riches of his grace in Christ Jesus. For this he has called us.

Paul says that these men of God were looking forward to these promises from afar, God having prepared something better for us. We have access to the riches of the glory of the inheritance of the saints. As we can see, apostles and prophets of God placed the foundation, of which Jesus is the cornerstone upon which we are built. Their lives are extremely eloquent, speaking to us of commitment, consecration, sanctification, and suffering. We are standing on the blood of the holy martyrs. Supporting this blessed inheritance is a combination of trials, sweat, tears, persecutions, insults, mocking from within and without, hunger, nakedness, imprisonments, beatings, knifings, loneliness and love. A love for the Lord that gives without reserve, for his glory. What can we say in response to this..., that we have filled the vacuum that they left when they disappeared from the scene of this world? Can we go on to eternity with the happy conviction that we have not defrauded the One who called us?

'Come with me, and I will make you fishers of men.' Can we hear this voice and still resist? This very day may you find no satisfaction in anything until you find the door that leads to being lost in God. He who loses his life for the sake of the Lord will find it, but he who wants to save his life will lose it. Being lost in God is to be found, and according to the measure of how much we give of ourselves, so shall we find. 'The secret of being and having is giving.'

In the silence of the sanctuary, in the communion of the saints or in the clamour of battle, never expect to receive more without having first given more. We will only have what we have given.

Chapter 2

I Looked For a Man

The earth has been and still is populated by millions. How is it that God could not find one man? The fact is that yesterday he searched and today he still searches. Not because no one person has ever been found since then, but because for each phase throughout generations he has raised up men in different parts of the world who spoke and acted in his name.

Ur of the Chaldees is visited. God, whose eyes of blazing fire range throughout the earth, found 'the man'. Who was he? A pagan from amongst so many living there. Abraham was called, blessed and multiplied in order to fulfil the divine plan (Isaiah 51:2).

The biographical reference by James concerning Elijah is striking. *'Elijah was a man....'* (James 5:17). Does he put it like this because we may think that there are no longer men of his calibre of faith? Or do we think that God will not do what he did before? Perhaps we do not consider ourselves able to release the infinite resources of God in this Great Work? What we can clearly understand, with great joy, is that all the servants of God were no more than ordinary men. They were made of the same material from which we are made, by the same God and with the same intent; that is to bring men to his feet and to have them live under his rule.

called, death, Moulded & Ministry

In moments of crisis the Lord of all the earth raised up a man. He called him, dealt with him, moulded him and gave him a ministry. He obeyed the voice of God, and God responded by breaking the laws of nature. *When God does everything that he has promised, it is because he has found a man who does everything that he wants*.

> *'I looked for a man among them who would build up the wall and stand before me in the gap on behalf of the land so that I would not have to destroy it, **but I found none.**'* (Ezekiel 22:30)

Really? Not even one soul whose heartbeat was in harmony with God's in his desire to save the suffering? Scripture is final: ***'I found none.'*** But remember Moses when he came down from the mountain with the tablets of the Law. What a contrast! A whole nation was to die for its sin. But here is the man of God. Look! He is standing in the gap between God and the people. Hear him speak to God, *'please forgive their sin – but if not, then blot me out of the book you have written.'* He put his life on the line to save his brothers. Few wish to put their life in such danger. Are we prepared to put our lives between a people and God, between a city and the powers of darkness, and not give up until it is saved? Is our own zeal like that of this man of God? The Lord was insisting,

> *'Now leave me alone so that my anger may burn against them and that I may destroy them. Then I will make you into a great nation.'* But Moses sought the favour of the LORD his God ... *'why should your anger burn against your people, whom you brought out of Egypt with great power and a mighty hand? Why should the Egyptians say "it was with evil intent that he brought them out to kill them in the mountains, and to wipe them off the face of the earth?" Turn from your*

14

> *fierce anger; relent and do not bring disaster on your people.'* (Exodus 32:1–35)

This earnest appeal caused the Lord to relent from his action.

It was wonderful to see how Moses was guided to the fire in the bush that was not burned up, and there God takes hold of him. Some time later we see the progress of Moses in his relationship with God. God says to a man *'leave me!'*, and now it is this man who takes hold of God. A little further on we again find something extraordinary in Exodus 33:12–22. Moses contends that he wants to see God. And there was Jehovah God, hearing the voice of his servant, in dialogue with him, knowing where he wanted to take him. God grants the request of this man who he loved more than anything.

> *'I will . . . cover you with my hand until I have passed by. Then I will remove my hand and you will see my back; but my face must not be seen.'* (Exodus 33:22–23)

Then later on, renewing the commission, God says to him:

> *'I am making a covenant with you. Before all your people I will do wonders never before done in any nation in all the world. The people you live among will see how awesome is the work that I, the LORD, will do for you.'* (Exodus 34:10)

How did Moses reach this position of privilege? What was it in him that so pleased God? Born in slavery, his life was saved by the holy fear of those midwives. Thrown out on to the perilous waters of the Nile, in danger until taken from the water, he got his name: 'Moses – Taken from the water'. Strange circumstances prevailed throughout his life. Not wanting human security he chose to live in the security of God, which is firmer than the strongest rock.

God Chooses the Things That Are Not

We have seen the call of God on the lives of these men over succeeding generations. Our father Abraham had nothing in the natural in which to glorify; nor did Moses, or Elijah. Amos too gives us his testimony (Amos 7:14–15), called from shepherding a flock of sheep to prophesy to a nation, being allowed to walk in the way of the servants of God. When God called Saul he too was a nobody, but the Lord anointed him to be king over the nation (1 Samuel 15:17).

Another exalted and haughty king proclaimed after his humiliation:

> *'the Most High is Sovereign over the kingdoms of men and gives them to anyone he wishes and sets over them the lowliest of men.'* (Daniel 4:17)

God says: 'You will be the head and not the tail' (Deuteronomy 28:13). He lifts the needy out of the dust and makes him sit in the place of princes (1 Samuel 2:8). Blessed be our God!

> *'Not many of* (us) *were wise by human standards; not many were influential; not many were of noble birth. But God chose the foolish things of the world to shame the wise; God chose the weak things of the world to shame the strong. He chose the lowly things of this world and the despised things – and the things that are not – to nullify the things that are, so that no-one may boast before him.'* (1 Corinthians 1:26–29)

Most of the disciples were unqualified and ordinary men.

Where did God get these Titans of the faith who changed the course of history? They were from a fishing village and from a tax booth. They were just jars of clay; so greater is the glory for him. What God chooses is not what we would think of.

Perhaps more than once your mind has been invaded by negative thoughts, and you have considered you were and still are a nobody in your own estimation. You measure your human ability, look at the undertaking and see how great it is, and you say 'I wasn't born for this'. Why calculate and measure up? It is God who measures, indeed he who measures the ocean in the palm of his hand and weighs the mountains on scales. Cast yourself into the arms of the Lord and he will sustain you! No matter how difficult the objective or how great the giant.

In Job 33:19–28, we find a picture that presents a challenge. It speaks of a man who is in agony and drying up little by little until he is at the verge of the grave.

> *'Yet if there is an angel on his side as a mediator, one out of a thousand, to tell a man what is right for him, to be gracious to him and say, "Spare him from going down to the pit; I have found a ransom for him" – then his flesh is renewed like a child's; it is restored as in the days of his youth. . . .* (he) *shall live to enjoy the light.'*
> (Job 33:23–25, 28)

Right now thousands around you are going down to the grave without experiencing Jesus in their life. Meanwhile God seeks a man who will stand in the gap on behalf of them so that they may not die. Will he find one in you? When I go to different places and see people in their sin, bound by Satan, ensnared in vice, slaves to sickness, crippled, it is as if I hear a cry: **'Please . . . , you who know God . . . , help us!'** Friend, what will we reply? Can we persist in our insensitivity? Jesus looked on the multitude and had compassion on them. What do you feel when you see the multitude?

Moses chose to be maltreated along with the people of God rather than enjoy the fleeting temporal delights of sin. He considered the reproach of Christ as greater riches than the treasure of the Egyptians. Let us come out too! ... leaving behind our social and religious comforts, so that if Christ had to begin his ministry today he would do nothing different from yesterday; travelling, always on the move, praying, fasting, preaching and healing the sick.

Chapter 3

The Wilderness

The wilderness is a desolate place, dry, dark, barren and uninhabited. There are great sectors of the Holy Land with a rainfall of only 50–80mm of rainfall per year. Plant and animal life are virtually nil in comparison with fertile land. There the juniper puts down its roots deep, penetrating the ground in search of the water that permits it to live.

The picture is of isolation and scarcity of resources where there is nothing you can put your hand to. God takes his men and his people again and again to the desert. Deuteronomy 8:2–4 records that there God afflicted his people, making them hunger, in order to know what was in their hearts. It was not, however, that he did not already know it; for it is we ourselves who need to know what is inside of us. We live in two extremes, too much or too little. We can think too highly of ourselves and our self-esteem becomes exaggerated. Our natural inclination is to look at the speck in another's eye and not see the beam in our own. Paul said,

> 'Do not think of yourself more highly than you ought, but rather think of yourself with sober judgment, in accordance with the measure of faith God has given you.'   (Romans 12:3)

Many people have a stunted spiritual life, thinking that they are all right, until they go out to face the wilderness and uncover the real truth of their state. Others need to be stripped for a while of those things in which they put their trust, in order to learn that man does not live by bread alone. In the desert one learns to depend entirely on God.

> *'Then they cried out to the Lord in their trouble, and he delivered them from their distress.'* (Psalm 107:4–9)

It is in the wilderness that we mature. The real measure of what we are is out there in the midst of the test. Jesus had only just been born and he had to cross the desert with his parents. Before receiving the approval of the Father to commence his ministry he was tempted and tested after forty days of fasting in the desert (Matthew 4:1). Then the miracles began to happen.

> *'Therefore I am now going to allure her; I will lead her into the desert and speak tenderly to her.'*
>
> (Hosea 2:14)

There in the dry land he gets to know us (Hosea 13:5). How difficult it is for us to be still, staying banished and hidden, but it is there that God speaks to our hearts. It is a great blessing to be surrounded by understanding brethren who can always give an answer to every need. We can grow in the shadow of their ministries, their lives supporting ours on many occasions; but if you really want to know God and if you do not want to live in mediocrity and second-hand experience, just being a loud-speaker which repeats all that it receives, living off borrowed experience, God will take you out to the desert.

Comforts Make Us Weak, Demands Make Us Strong

Our father Abraham left without knowing where he was going, leaving civilisation and walking the length and breadth of the land, with no fixed abode. From him would come a nation, including the Messiah, and all the descendants of the earth would be blessed in him. It was a very great honour, but it had its price. On reading about his life we find the footprints of God's dealings with him; the formation of a man made in divine insecurity. The results were positive; he had a purified faith.

One of the tragedies we face is the loss of faith. How easily we get deflated! But this man was not like that. The writer of the letter to the Romans says:

> *'Without weakening in his faith, he faced the fact that his body was as good as dead – since he was about a hundred years old – and that Sarah's womb was also dead. Yet he did not waver through unbelief regarding the promise of God, but was strengthened in his faith and gave glory to God, being fully persuaded that God had power to do what he had promised.'*

(Romans 4:19–21)

He did not just maintain his faith but was strengthened in it more and more, being fully convinced of God's faithfulness. When fears and doubts assailed him, when the impossible reality struck him in the face, he lifted his thoughts to God, with his eyes open to the dimension of the Spirit, he contemplated a majestic, omnipotent, omniscient, omnipresent, unshakeable God, who knows all things and can do all things! And he began to give glory and praise until he reached still greater levels of faith. This faith and this obedience brought about the long awaited Isaac.

In Galatians 5:22 we find faith as a fruit of the Spirit. In 1 Corinthians 12:9 it appears as a gift given by the Spirit. The former is that in which we grow and express like trees of God, for without faith it is impossible to please God. The latter is not produced by the tree, rather it is given as a gift on the tree. The gift of faith is to believe for those unable to believe. Biblical examples show that many were released by their own faith, whilst others like the paralytic found by Peter and John were released by the faith of those who ministered to them. The wilderness produces men of such a disposition.

Elijah was a man approved by God. God used him in a time of decadence and moral and spiritual confusion. His message was dogmatic and forceful. Resolute and full of fire, this prophet was a restorer of law and order. He had to confront the powers of darkness with the power of God. Miracles, marvels, healings, signs and wonders took place when he released the resources of God for the work. Just one man was enough for God to bring upheaval to the whole nation. They looked for him in distant lands without finding him. He shut the skies, opened them again, rebuked the king, destroyed the prophets of Baal after praying down fire from heaven. But meanwhile he had to pass through the school of God. Ravens had to feed him until the stream dried up. He constantly faced danger and needs. Fed by a widow, it did not trouble his conscience to eat the last meal she had. Even the chosen believers would criticise him today. What many do not understand is that there would be no work of God without a worker. In this respect the worker is the most important for God. This is why neither he nor the widow nor her son were in need while others died of hunger. God takes first place in the order of priorities. We must have God in the foreground, the word of God cannot be postponed, and our obedience releases the power held therein.

Returning to Elijah once again. Tired, persecuted, hungry, thirsty..., he crossed the desert. The moment came when he could no longer go on and he fell down wanting to die right there. God was dealing with him and we remember that he did not see death; his ministry needed to continue. Only this way can we be tried and approved. The desert will not be the grave of the man of God who suffers in his cause. There will always be a cake and a jar of water sent by an angel of God, even when we are in the midst of the wilderness. God is a specialist in things impossible. The life of this servant of God is recorded in 1 Kings 17:1–2 Kings 2:13.

John the Baptist also lived and ministered in the desert. His ministry melted consciences and drove the people's hearts to remorse, his appeal was inescapable.

What did these men have? They did not have our technology, nor did they have the media or our means of travel. However, like Jesus, they stood in one place and the multitudes came to them. There was a powerful magnet in them that attracted the people who just by hearing their names could not resist seeing and hearing them.

Saint Paul, another man of solitude, was three years hidden after he had been called. He did not consult flesh and blood. Those who seemed to be important gave him nothing. Where did he learn so much? It was he who gave the building its shape. Half of the New Testament is taken up by his letters. Who taught him? He said,

> *'I know a man in Christ who fourteen years ago ... whether in the body or apart from the body I do not know, but God knows – was caught up to Paradise. He heard inexpressible things, things that man is not permitted to tell.'*   (2 Corinthians 12:2–4)

Three years of wilderness produced this giant. God + desert = valiant men. In beatings, imprisonments, persecutions, hunger and thirst, lack of sleep, nakedness, criticism, shipwrecks, danger from bandits and from his own countrymen, sickness, stonings; he went through the wilderness (2 Corinthians 11:23–33, 12:1–10). He never gave up! He stayed firm in God, strong and courageous.

To begin with we said that God takes us to the desert to face ourselves. When we have counted ourselves dead, when we have not given up, then the Lord can grow in us. It took forty years looking after sheep in the desert of Midian to erase all human capacity out of Moses. That strong young man who could knock down a bigger opponent had to flee in a hurry. Now he had neither sword nor spear in his hand. When God called him he asked, *'What is that in your hand?'* (Exodus 4:2). He showed him the shepherd's staff – a dry stick. That was all that was necessary, with it he would loose ten plagues upon Egypt and do miracles in the desert; opening up the Red Sea, drawing water from the hard rock. He left the flock to go and challenge the Pharaoh. How inexplicable for the human mind! Just the opposite of what men do.

Imagine him, his hair and clothes blowing in the wind, looking to the Invisible for support. The people wait facing the sea ... behind them is the enemy army, whose shouting and the clamour of their chariots and horses draws ever closer ... there is this giant of God. He is only a man, no more, but he is in the hand of God. The waters opened and the people crossed over on a dry path. The turbulent mass of water then closed in torrents to swallow up their enemies.

John the apostle knew Jesus personally. He saw him spend many nights in prayer, days in fasting, all the time on the move, comforting, healing and delivering. He knew the Preacher of the Good News, the Saviour, the Healer, the Deliverer, he who raised the dead; but even John did not know him completely. It was when for his sake that he was exiled in Patmos, there in the solitude of that island, in need and facing the danger of death, already ageing and seeming that the time had come for him to leave this world, he received his Great Revelation: Jesus, King of kings and Lord of lords. It did not come when his hands could touch him, nor in splendid ministry. No, it was in the wilderness, humanly defenceless, that humble fisherman wrote what even today the most erudite and elevated theologians cannot interpret.

Yes, friend..., when we no longer have crutches nor even a stick to lean on, when we are cut off in our exile, in solitude, going through barrenness and dryness, with no provision and when nobody seems to remember us, it is as if God and men have abandoned us. Never complain or rebel. Send your roots down good and deep in search of water ... yes..., there is living water to be found in these hard times. Of course it is not superficial, it is a profound experience in God. Christ was abandoned by God and men when he exclaimed: 'Father, why have you abandoned me?' The psalmist says of him:

> *'I am like a desert owl, like an owl among the ruins. I lie awake; I have become like a bird alone on a roof.'*
> (Psalm 102:6–7)

When the warm blood began to trickle down his face, life ebbing from his wounds, his disciples abandoned him. Where were the multitudes that he had fed? Where were the blind, lame, and sick who had been healed, and the dead he had brought to life? All of them had abandoned him. Man of sorrows, tested and broken. Even his Father left him for a time when he loaded all the filth of sin on to him.

All these men of God went out to take classes in the Great Hall of the Theological Faculty of the Wilderness. They are the illustrious students who graduated to challenge Satan and his retinue.

Other Results

Thousands of souls yielded different results. Today it happens just the same. Whilst there are those who in the desert receive great revelation, anointing and ministries, others fail in their time of testing.

> *'In the desert they gave in to their craving; in the wasteland they put God to the test. So he gave them what they asked for, but sent a wasting disease upon them ... Then they despised the pleasant land; they did not believe his promise. They grumbled in their tents and did not obey the Lord. So he swore to them with uplifted hand that he would make them fall in the desert.'* (Psalm 106:14–15, 24–26)

> *'See to it, brothers, that none of you has a sinful, unbelieving heart that turns away from the living God ... And with whom was he angry for forty years? Was it not with those who sinned, whose bodies fell in the desert? And to whom did God swear that they would never enter his rest if not to those who disobeyed? So we see that thy were not able to enter, because of their unbelief.'* (Hebrews 3:12, 17–19)

Their bones were left to bleach in the desert.

Jesus was with his disciples and a great multitude in a remote place (Luke 9:10–17). They faced a need as it was days since the people had eaten. A young boy who had been amongst the crowd brought to Jesus five loaves and two fishes. The people had to settle, lie down and rest so they could be witnesses of a great miracle. Five thousand men, without counting women and children, ate on that day and twelve baskets of pieces were left over.

What is Put into the Hands of Jesus

If that frugal provision had not been placed into the hands of the Lord, if it had been consumed there would have been enough for just one person once. If he had kept it in his bag it would have been wasted to no benefit. But neither happened. In the hands of Jesus it was broken, blessed and distributed.

When we are in the desert we discover just how little we have to offer to Jesus. Don't be discouraged. Even though it is little, put it into the hands of the Lord. Rest and observe your Lord do great miracles with your life and through your life. By his Word was made everything that can be seen, from what cannot be seen. The prophet knew the power of these words:

> *'Though the fig-tree does not bud and there are no grapes on the vines, though the olive crop fails and the fields produce no food, though there are no sheep in the pen and no cattle in the stalls, yet I will rejoice in the Lord, I will be joyful in God my Saviour.'*
>
> (Habakkuk 3:17–18)

Yes . . . , by his Word he can create what does not yet exist.

Who is this coming up from the desert with the fragrance of the anointing?

Who is this coming up from the desert leaning on her lover? It is the glorious Church of the Lord, illustrious and imposing, anointed, coming out approved from the desert. She has honoured her Lord and Head. Jesus said:

> *'My Father will honour the one who serves me.'*
>
> (John 12:26)

27

This is the way of those who have come through the great tribulation and have washed their robes and made them white in the blood of the Lamb.

Chapter 4

Knowing God

There are three aspects of knowledge that we need to have. This knowledge is not the product of reason, intelligence or human wisdom. It is something superior.

We cannot grow, much less serve, without the initial revelation of the person of God. Our eyes have to be opened to see him in the dimension of the Spirit. We must see his person and his character. This is fundamental knowledge.

We may know the clearly defined will of God by learning from the scriptures. God never changed his plans. Revelation remains unchanged. All that we must be and do for God has already been made clear. The foundation of apostles and prophets is immovable, nobody may lay any other foundation (1 Corinthians 3:11). Comprehension of it may be widened and deepened but it may never be changed or modified. Apart from this, for every child of God there is a purpose which is unique and special. God does not have moulds into which he fits one or another. So the need arises for the knowledge of his will for many steps in our lives. This is another aspect of knowledge.

A person who knows God will know that without fail, his purposes and will have a commission to fulfil. God does not reveal anything without a purpose. Paul says:

> '*God ... was pleased to reveal his Son in me so that I might preach him among the Gentiles ... '*
>
> (Galatians 1:14–16)

When we take proper stock of the work to be accomplished we then face the needs in both the spiritual and the material realm. For these we bend the knee before God, asking him for his provision and his power in our work. Would you be surprised if I said that the provision **has already been made** beforehand? Our eyes should be opened to this knowledge of the inexhaustible supplies of divine resources to carry out the commission which God has given us. So:

(a)   Know God
(b)   Know his purposes
(c)   Know his resources

With such a revelation a faithful and obedient man may revolutionise the world and change it for the glory of God. What we can do for God is not so important as what he can do through us. Every child of God has a tremendous power inside – the power of the Holy Spirit – God himself in us.

Amos declares:

> '*Surely the Sovereign* LORD *does nothing without revealing his plan to his servants the prophets.*'
>
> (Amos 3:7)

And the Lord says:

> '*You are my friends if you do what I command. I no longer call you servants, because a servant does not know his master's business.*'   (John 15:14–15)

Abraham was the friend of God. This friendship enabled Abraham to intercede for the saving of other lives. God was about to destroy the sinful cities of Sodom and Gomorrah, and said:

> *'Shall I hide from Abraham what I am about to do?'*
> (Genesis 18:17)

God knows how to be a friend.

> *'A friend loves at all times, and a brother is born for adversity.'* (Proverbs 17:17)

> *'A man who has friends must himself be friendly, but there is a friend who sticks closer than a brother.'*
> (Proverbs 18:24 NKJV)

More than servants, God wants us to be his friends. He will never do anything without first communicating with his friends.

We have seen that men and women in the Bible and in modern times could know God more through their moments of suffering. We do not like to face these times of crisis, but generally they are the golden gate through which the Lord appears, coming to our aid and showing us something more of himself. On the sea of Galilee the startled disciples saw that they were on the point of capsizing. They had done all they could and now could do no more. Jesus went into action and everything went calm. 'Who is this that even the wind and the sea obey?' Until then they had seen nothing like this. It was necessary for them to pass through an experience of being helpless and desperate for them to learn this lesson.

There are two types of suffering: one is according to the world and is for death; the other is according to God and gives life. When some situation gives us pain for the sake of the Lord let us stay close to him, for we are approaching the door that leads us to another dimension of the knowledge of God.

Men who were formed like this on the anvil of faith, in the living fire of testings, formed like the lampstand of gold which was wrought blow by blow with the hammer, are able to light up the darkness and be used in the sanctuary (Exodus 25:31). We need this knowledge too.

> *'Where there is no vision, the people perish.'*
> (Proverbs 29:18 KJV)

> *'My people are destroyed from lack of knowledge.'*
> (Hosea 4:6)

> *'For I desire mercy, not sacrifice, and acknowledgment of God rather than burnt offerings.'* (Hosea 6:6)

Vision allows us to know, always perceiving that there is a purpose.

> *'Though it linger wait for it; it will certainly come and will not delay.'* (Habakkuk 2:3)

The light that comes to us from God places us in a responsible position. We are committed. It is at this point that men fail. From here on we have to take decisions that will cost us dearly. There are those who do not want to pay the price. Barak said to Balaam:

> *'I said I would reward you handsomely, but the Lord has kept you from being rewarded.'* (Numbers 24:11)

This king was thinking of remunerating the prophet, but since the man insisted on obeying the Lord he would lose his reward. In any case things turned out badly for him because he disobeyed in another way. He did not remain faithful. We have to maintain our faithfulness to the

Lord, even though it costs us. When a person has established a standard of conduct in the Lord he will be misunderstood, lose honour, and some friends will no longer see him as they used to. You cannot please men and God at the same time. Our relationships, all of them, are in the Lord. And according to the flesh we do not even know Christ. The servant cannot be greater than his master, and Jesus had two types of people who followed him; those who wanted to make him king and those who wanted to kill him. The servant of God is the most loved and the most hated. We should tremble if all speak well of us. For this reason many children of God have closed the door on the work of the Holy Spirit. It didn't suit them because they had too much to lose. Just like many Pharisees in the time of Jesus; they knew that he was the Messiah but it did not suit them to recognise it. And the people of God? They will perish without a vision! They will be destroyed for lack of knowledge! May God forgive us this sin. How are we going to have success in our work for God? Everything that is done like this **does not have God's backing**. I have heard prayers in public asking for the will of God for his church, and when it came they pretended to be deaf and distracted. Then later they weep. What is the value of tears shed in this way? God wants us to cry less and obey him more. Why carry on with more prayers? God will not send anybody else to speak to us on his behalf when he knows that we will not pay any attention! **Let us not be cowards**, and let us go on with the Lord whatever the consequences. For this purpose God is calling his people to repentance in this time; beginning with those in leadership in the inheritance of the Lord.

> '"Even now", declares the LORD, "return to me with all your heart, with fasting and weeping and mourning." ... declare a holy fast, call a sacred assembly. Gather the people, consecrate the assembly; bring

together the elders, gather the children, those nursing at the breast ... Let the priests, who minister before the LORD, *weep between the temple porch and the altar. Let them say, "Spare your people, O* LORD. *Do not make your inheritance an object of scorn, a byword among the nations. Why should they say among the peoples, 'Where is their God?'"'*   (Joel 2:12–17)

The Reproach of God

'Woe to the worthless shepherd, who deserts the flock! May the sword strike his arm and his right eye! May his arm be completely withered, his right eye totally blinded!'   (Zechariah 11:17)

'Woe to the shepherds of Israel who only take care of themselves! Should not shepherds take care of the flock? You eat the curds, clothe yourselves with the wool and slaughter the choice animals, but you do not take care of the flock. You have not strengthened the weak or bound up the injured. You have not brought back the strays or searched for the lost. You have ruled them harshly and brutally. So they were scattered because there was no shepherd, and when they were scattered they became food for all the wild animals. My sheep wandered over all the mountains and on every high hill. They were scattered over the whole earth, and no-one searched or looked for them. . . . This is what the Sovereign LORD *says: I am against the shepherds and will hold them accountable for my flock.'*   (Ezekiel 34:2–10)

'The shepherds are senseless and do not enquire of the LORD; *so they do not prosper and all their flock is scattered.'*   (Jeremiah 10:21)

> ' *"And now this admonition is for you, O priests. If you do not listen, and if you do not set your heart to honour my name," says the* LORD *Almighty, "I will send a curse upon you, and I will curse your blessings. Yes, I have already cursed them, because you have not set your heart to honour me." '* (Malachi 2:1–2)

'Where is my honour?' asks God. Anything will do for God, so they presented to him the blemished sheep, the poorest and the leftovers for God, this is what they offered him and pretended to please him (Malachi 1:6–8).

Beloved, things are not so different today. How can the Lord send something greater for our land? Perhaps fire will fall, but not from the Holy Spirit. Not the fire of purification but a consuming fire. The fires of hell will be the consequence of our lack of the fire from God.

> ' *... they all turn to their own way, each seeks his own gain.* ' (Isaiah 56:11)

It is time to stop in our tracks and examine our condition. It is time to stop pushing at the door which is shut and getting left with the handle in our hand. Why? –

> '*The ox knows his master, the donkey his owner's manger, but Israel does not know, my people do not understand.*' (Isaiah 1:3)

How many things are done without God's direction! We use unauthorised fire for the Lord. We depend on men and not God for support. I believe that we have to humble ourselves, weep and wail, fast and lament so that God will include us and not pass us by.

Seeking to Know Him Better

Prayer is the key that opens the heavens. Saint Paul prayed that his brothers would receive from the glorious Father, the Spirit of wisdom and revelation, so that they would know him better. And that the eyes of their heart would be enlightened, in order that they would know the hope to which they were called, the riches of his glorious inheritance in the saints (Ephesians 1:14–18). *Purpos*

> *'And this is my prayer: that your love may abound more and more in knowledge and depth of insight, so that you may be able to discern what is best and may be pure and blameless until the day of Christ.'*
>
> (Philippians 1:9–10)

The prayer is accompanied by an attitude; Paul gives his testimony:

> *'But whatever was to my profit I now consider loss for the sake of Christ. What is more, I consider everything a loss compared to the surpassing greatness of knowing Christ Jesus my Lord, for whose sake I have lost all things. I consider them rubbish, that I may gain Christ, and be found in him, not having a righteousness of my own that comes from the law, but that which is through faith in Christ – the righteousness that comes from God and is by faith. I want to know Christ and the power of his resurrection and the fellowship of sharing in his sufferings, becoming like him in his death, and so, somehow, to attain to the resurrection from the dead.'*
>
> (Philippians 3:7–11)

We have to send everything that is not of the Father to the rubbish tip, and he will give us a higher knowledge: the filling of the knowledge of his will through *'all spiritual wisdom and understanding'* (Colossians 1:9–10).

Unity and love are the factors which lead to full knowledge of the mystery of God the Father and of Christ . . .
*'in whom are hidden all the treasures of wisdom and know-
ledge'* (Colossians 2:2–3).

Visions of God

*'I saw the Lord seated on a throne, high and exalted,
and the train of his robe filled the temple . . . Holy,
holy, holy is the LORD Almighty; the whole earth is full
of his glory. At the sound of their voices the doorposts
and the thresholds shook and the temple was filled with
smoke.'*   (Isaiah 6:1–4)

*'The Lord has established his throne in heaven, and his
kingdom rules over all.'*   (Psalm 103:19)

Let us look at this together with them:

*'No-one is like you, O LORD; you are great, and your
name is mighty in power. Who should not revere you, O
King of the nations? This is your due . . . **there is no-one
like you**.'*   (Jeremiah 10:6–7)

*'And I saw the glory of the God of Israel coming from
the east. His voice was like the roar of rushing waters,
and the land was radiant with his glory.'*

(Ezekiel 43:2).

*'The Lord, the LORD Almighty, he who touches the
earth and it melts.'*   (Amos 9:5)

*'Look! the Lord is coming out from his dwelling-place;
he comes down and treads the high places of the earth.
The mountains melt beneath him and the valleys split
apart like wax before the fire,'*   (Micah 1:3–4)

> *'His throne was flaming with fire, ... Thousands upon thousands attended him.'* (Daniel 7:9–10)

Read the song of Miriam when they crossed the Red Sea; and the song of Moses. The song of Deborah; the song of Habakkuk; the songs of David. The song of Mary mother of Jesus, and many other giants of God. Their visions of God were great and powerful. When God came down on Mount Sinai the earth trembled, everything was shaken, with fire and smoke and resplendent glory, in such a way that the children of Israel were terrified.

May the veil be drawn back from our eyes so that God may amaze and astonish us! The earth is shaken in space like a particle of cosmic dust, and by his breath is destruction. Who can hold back his hand? Who can block his way? Is anything too difficult for him? Anything impossible? Who has seen, who has heard, what mind conceived? Captain of the hosts and Man of war! **This is our God! See him with eyes of faith!** Open our eyes that we may behold him and exalt him! Proclaim his great and terrible name! Blessed be our merciful and forgiving God throughout all ages, Holy Redeemer!

As we grow in our knowledge of God we will find that his personality grows greater and greater, while ours gets smaller and smaller. The greater our vision of the person of God, the smaller we will see ourselves. When a man is great in God then he is indeed small.

Let us pray, seeking to know God more, and to know his purposes and to know his resources. The Lord is widening our vision and is stretching us in action.

Chapter 5

The Dimension of the Kingdom

'The God who gives life to the dead and calls things that are not as though they were.' (Romans 4:17)

'So we fix our eyes not on what is seen, but on what is unseen. For what is seen is temporary, **but what is unseen is eternal.**' (2 Corinthians 4:18)

'The man without the Spirit does not accept the things that come from the Spirit of God, for they are foolishness to him, and he cannot understand them, because they are spiritually discerned.' (1 Corinthians 2:14)

The divine ideal can only live when we move within the orbit of the Holy Spirit.

There are two kinds of view: the spiritual and the natural view. People generally, and even a vast sector of Christians, live, talk, think and act in conformity to outward things. Their reasoning and feelings show us that their lives are governed by what they can see and touch. From here we get our saying: 'Seeing is believing'. They live in the kingdom of man. The new life that we have received from God should and must be lived out in the spirit. Hearing, thinking, doing and seeing in the spirit. Only in this way can we say that we are walking in the kingdom of God. Our spirit was joined to the Spirit of

Christ and we were given life, we were renewed. There is now a power and a potential working within us. If we could become fully conscious of what this means we would discover that we are able to overcome the limitations of our outer man. And if the Spirit of him who raised Jesus from the dead is dwelling within us, then by faith our mortal bodies will be brought to life.

This is the operation of the Holy Spirit in us. Our spirit must live in continual renewal; and so it is strengthened day by day. Meditation on the Word of God, praise and adoration are exercises which contribute to the growth of the fruit of the Spirit; an abundant fruit in our lives.

We have to recognise that in the field of spiritual things we know very little. Some years ago the Lord showed us things about the occurrence of a spiritual revival. Millions would find a new life in the spiritual dimension. Multitudes would find life in Christ, but lamentably many would be shipwrecked in their spiritual life through their connections with the powers of darkness. As time goes by we are seeing that it is just how God showed us it would be. Spiritualist practices which appear under various different names are poisoning souls who are thirsty for spiritual life. Mankind is tired of struggling with his own limitations, and is seeking something beyond the natural; something that offers a life which is raised above the material. Thousands of souls open the doors of their minds and spirits to be possessed by foul spirits. In their ignorance they are increasingly misled into a paranormal world, manipulating and being manipulated by unseen and unknown powers which sooner or later, as Jesus says, steal, kill and destroy their victims. Is this not a challenge? These unhappy souls are going to drink this poison, opening themselves up to demons. Would you not like to open yourself up to the Holy Spirit? Minister, Christian, worker; will you through prejudice keep the doors closed to the Holy Spirit? Should we not persevere at the feet of the Lord for a filling that will impart power from on high to others?

Eloquent Testimonies

Men of God from other times conversed directly with God, they saw the angels of God and spoke with them (Genesis 12:7). Genesis chapter 18 relates something that today even the chosen Christians would not believe. The angels went to Sodom and Gomorrah and were there to rescue Lot. When they took on human appearance, those men of God could understand and converse with them, because they had spiritual understanding.

Remember Balaam when he stubbornly argued against the will of God which he had already been shown. Even though the donkey had seen the angel, he was too blind to see. He talked with the animal and discussed the question of obedience. Until God opened his eyes he didn't know what was going on, and if the donkey had not left the road the prophet would have died. She saved his life. Later on, having already fallen, he could now see in the spiritual realm but he could not participate in the blessing. Fallen, but his eyes now opened! (Numbers 24). In his parable he prophesied the victory of Israel. He prophesied concerning the Messiah. He uttered tremendous blessing upon the tents of Israel. Later on he died by the sword at the hands of the same people whom he had blessed.

It is important to have our eyes open to the spiritual realm and to understand the vision, but that is not the end of it. We have to be part of that vision, integrated into its purpose. The worker is in one sense also the work. Paul says:

> '... *so that after I have preached to others, I myself will not be disqualified for the prize,*'
>
> (1 Corinthians 9:27)

and

> *'I press on towards the goal to win the prize for which
> God has called me heavenwards in Christ Jesus.'*
>
> (Philippians 3:14)

Seeing but Not Perceiving, Hearing but Not Understanding

Elisha was in Dothan (2 Kings 6:13–17). The king of Syria had besieged the city. When the servant of the man of God saw the army he cried out in fright. *'Oh my Lord what shall we do?'* This man could only see with his natural sight; though looking, he could not see. The man of God had to pray for him. When his eyes were opened to the spiritual realm he noticed that they were not alone. The interesting thing is that this provision of God for protection did not come about through Elisha's prayer. It was already there. The company of God was there all the time. It was an army superior to natural forces.

The angels of God encamp around those who fear and love the God who defends them. We are not properly aware, but we are surrounded by a spiritual world which affects our spirits and even the material things of this world. Our lack of knowledge about these things is bad enough, but the tragedy is that we fail to recognise or give any importance to them. Jesus called the religious men of his time 'blind guides'. If the blind leads the blind, both will fall into a pit. They look but do not see. They listen but do not hear. Today there is still much spiritual short-sightedness. May God anoint our eyes with spiritual salve so that we may see our distress and our afflictions. May we see our nakedness so that we may be clothed as the Lord would have us. Let us be refined gold; paying the price! Let us break out from lukewarmness and see with spiritual eyes the Kingdom of the Father.

Firm – Immovable

'Therefore, since we are receiving a kingdom that cannot be shaken, let us be thankful, and so worship God acceptably with reverence and awe, for our "God is a consuming fire." ' (Hebrews 12:28–29)

'I know that everything God does will endure for ever; nothing can be added to it and nothing taken from it. God does it so that men will revere him.

Whatever is has already been, and what will be has been before; and God will call the past to account.'
(Ecclesiastes 3:14–15)

The Kingdom of Heaven has come to men. We have learnt that the Kingdom of God is the divine rule over men. Jesus is the greatest ruler of all, King and Lord of his Kingdom. He brought us new life, a life dictated by spiritual values. This is a law; the law of the Spirit of life in Christ Jesus. We have been born of the Spirit and must live by the Spirit. It is the only way to please God. No longer do we feel our way along but now we go on with confidence. By faith and not by sight. By faith in Jesus and in his Word. Jesus brought the Kingdom of the Father to men and women. In this Kingdom there are certain orders, demands and expectancies but there is provision as well. There are riches in glory, of which we have become administrators. This is the immovable Kingdom. The divine resources do not come as a result of praying, rather they are released by our prayer. Like the army in Dothan, they are already here. They always were, from the time when Jesus exclaimed from the cross: *'It is finished'*. In other words, **it has all been done**. He saved us, we died with him, by his wounds he healed us, he cleansed us, forgave us and we were raised with him. All we have to do is to believe that this is so, taking it by faith. When we obey the words of God their power is released for us. God's resources are loosed upon those who believe and obey. If Naaman had dipped himself only six times in the Jordan he would not have been healed of his leprosy. But he was healed after the seventh time, as the man of God had said.

Christ was made our provision by our Father God. He is the complete fulfilment of all things. He will not come again to do anything else for us; he has already done it all. In him we are complete and in the power of his name all things are released. The King and his kingdom, together with all the assets of his great government, are now here amongst us. His Person and his resources are without limit. We live with mere fragments of the whole of what God is and has for us. He is immeasurable. We faint, we tremble, we yearn and crave, because we do not see with spiritual eyes the glorious presence of God and all his great resources.

We do not heal the sick, rather we pray for God to heal them, for God to save them, to give them his love, peace and patience. We fail to understand that God **already gave us everything in Christ**. Why do we go on searching? Because we fail to know where everything is. We do not see it and so we ask for it. When we see it we will no longer ask, we will confidently go and take it because it is already ours, **it has already been given to us**.

That which was now is; and that which will be has already been. All we have to do is to discover it in Christ. God will restore what has gone by. What was lived in other times has been repeated in various men of different generations. But now God is **restoring all** and is **renewing** with even greater glory than that which went before. If the beginning was glorious then the closing eras will not be less so. Ananias talked to the Holy Spirit when he was sent to pray for Paul. The apostles raised the dead, released the demon possessed, and healed the sick, as they extended and established the Kingdom of God, the Lord confirming the preaching of the Word with signs and wonders.

God is restoring us and renewing us, that the latter glory may be greater than the former. May God open our eyes so that once and for all we will not muddle and puzzle our way along! May we be endued with a greater capability, so that we may minister to other souls all that he has provided.

Chapter 6

The Design

There is power in the blood of Jesus. In the natural, blood
has antibodies which function to perfection. All that is not
of the body or for the body will be rejected, and materials
foreign to its design will not prosper. The blood of Jesus
works in his Body, the Church, refusing admission to
undesirable elements by the absolute faithfulness of the
Holy Spirit. Are we able to rest in this truth? Will the
Spirit of God be faithful to carry out the sacred commission to build the Church? By the attitude of thousands of
Christians it would seem that his function is placed in
doubt. Theoretically and intellectually they assert the
truth of the scriptures in this respect, but in practice it is
another matter.

The Ministry of the Holy Spirit

> *'And I will ask the Father, and he will give you another
> Counsellor to be with you for ever – the Spirit of truth.'*
> (John 14:16)

> *'But the Counsellor, the Holy Spirit, whom the Father
> will send in my name, will teach you all things and will
> remind you of everything I have said to you.'*
> (John 14:26)

> '... *he will testify about me.'* (John 15:26)

> '*he will guide you into all truth ... and he will tell you what is yet to come.'* (John 16:13)

He is the Comforter, he is the Truth, he teaches, reminds, guides, testifies about Christ, he knows beforehand what will happen and goes ahead, revealing all (1 Corinthians 2:12–16).

> '*The Spirit searches all things, even the deep things of God.'* (1 Corinthians 2:10)

> '*The Spirit helps us in our weakness. We do not know what we ought to pray for, but the Spirit himself intercedes for us with groans that words cannot express.'* (Romans 8:26)

This is the only prayer that Satan is unable to interrupt, speaking mysteries only understood by God and edifying the Christian.

> '*"Not by might nor by power, but by my Spirit," says the Lord Almighty.'* (Zechariah 4:6)

Are we able to trust and believe these words? Why is it that we do not see the fullness of this blessed ministry in our lives? If the Holy Spirit is faithful, if he will never fail in his mission, then there are things in us that have to be broken so that the flow of God may surpass the limited capacity of our imagination. Just as Jerusalem was restored from the dust and rubble, so the Lord of the Church is restoring all things within her. The days are coming when his glory will overflow like a river bursting its banks. Only the Holy Spirit can lead us to a realisation of all things according to the mind of God, according to his will and desire.

When God gave Moses the design of the tabernacle (Exodus 24–27), he called him to go up the mountain. Moses had to enter into the cloud of glory which had settled on Mount Sinai and looked like a consuming fire. He was there for forty days and forty nights, receiving every tiny detail of all that had to be done. God left nothing free to human criteria. It is man who must adapt to God and his ways, not God to the plans of man. Intellectual and gifted Christians make their plans and programmes, and then ask God to associate with them and bless what they have devised. The Lord has to move according to their requirements, and at the time they consider it necessary. If not they don't even pray; in any case they know it all! In such plans there is no room for God. God has no interest in them either. He will **not support them**, despite their natural abilities, gifts and talents. God searched out men of his choice and filled them with his Spirit, with skill, ability and knowledge to carry out the work of constructing the sanctuary. He did not just reveal the design. Since it was a project from above, they could not work with the natural mind. They needed the filling and direction of the Holy Spirit (Exodus 35:30–35).

It is inspiring to read the words that narrate what happened in the different stages of the work. Moses did what God had commanded, and the sons of Israel also did what God had decreed through Moses. The writer of the letter to the Hebrews mentions the excellence of our Great High Priest, and speaks of the earthly tabernacle. However, even though its design and purpose came as a revelation from God for his service, this tabernacle was a shadow of what was to come. So if even in the imperfect it was necessary to observe faithfully everything that was ordered by God, being filled with the Spirit of wisdom and knowledge, how much more is it necessary in the sanctuary of living stones that is built upon the

cornerstone, Stone of salvation and Stone of stumbling?
(1 Peter 2:4–8).

It is not possible to do anything in the Spirit with the
carnal mind. So do you now see why there are so many
failures? But we have the mind of Christ.

In many cases the organisation has devoured the organism. The body of Christ is a structured organism, but it is
not an organisation. In one there is life but the other is a
system. Many men who started well were trapped and
devoured by the religious system. They value their ecclesi-
astical duties and use their positions to favour those who
oblige them. Others will not speak the truth for fear of the
whole thing falling apart. They want to preserve the struc-
tures with indulgences and arrangements that in other
times would have been in no way acceptable. They have
to swallow their inner convictions which were in accordance with what God says, because if they were to follow
them they would come against their friends and col-
leagues. They do not realise that in the end they will fall
anyway. God has no interest in making a greater system
or a conglomerate, even though it may have been effective
in another time. God is establishing his kingdom. We are
and should be establishing the Kingdom of God. God is
forming a **people**; one people, not two or more. It is hard
for us to accept change, but we must let the Holy Spirit
work and take us to where God would lead. If not we will
get left behind like museum pieces; others will take our
place and will do what we did not want to. We will regret
it but will surely see it happen.

With music and song, tambourine and dance, with
clamour and celebration, the sons of Israel brought the
ark of God up on a new ox-cart. David, a man who loved
God, was coming up at the front of the procession. When
the oxen stumbled Uzzah reached out to steady the ark
and was struck down dead (2 Samuel 6:7). So David
asked the question that he should have asked in the first

place. *'How can I ever bring the ark of God to me?'* (1 Chronicles 13:12).

> *'Then David said: "No-one but the Levites may carry the ark of God, because the LORD chose them to carry the ark of the LORD and to minister before him for ever ... It was because you, the Levites, did not bring it up the first time that the LORD our God broke out in anger against us. We did not enquire of him about how to do it in the prescribed way." '*   (1 Chronicles 15:2, 13)

Yes, it has to be just like God says or there will be death instead of life.

We have learned that God wants neither guests nor volunteers, rather those who are called and sent. This too has brought great problems to the church of the Lord. People with good intentions, who want to teach what they have learned, who without doubt love God, but who unfortunately are just volunteers and so yield negative results. It is not a question of inviting an able and eloquent Bible expositor, nor receiving him as a volunteer. It has to be one who has a **calling**, one who has been **sent**. In God's timing, in the place of God's choosing, together with those men whom God has called and sent. This way it all becomes so simple; and **all** the much hoped for things are achieved.

No more volunteers, no more guests but people who are called, tested and approved. God has his men in every country. They will be sent out, the mighty men of God's army. We have to leave the fertile plain and go up to the arid and rocky places of the mountain, enter into the cloud of glory and, once there, to wait for precise instructions from God. We need to hear from God. We need to hear, because even our prayers spring from a mind that makes suggestions, reproaches and therefore offends God. 'Do not abandon us Lord ... ,' seems to be the pious prayer of a woman. Have you ever heard from the mouth of a Christian anything more contrary to the revealed truth of God? Well, there are many prayers of that kind. Did not the Lord say: 'Never will I leave you, never will I forsake you?' May God clear such negative and human ideas out of our minds!

There are birds that make their nests in the field. They lay their eggs to hatch their chicks. When they leave the nest to find food, and on their return find that someone has touched their eggs they break them and go somewhere else, making a new nest to lay their eggs and rear their young. The sheer sensitivity of these birds has more than once made me think of the work of the Holy Spirit. The Spirit is he who gives life to the church. If we read of the life of the church we will find out about the moving of the Spirit in different groups. A spark from God was ignited in them and they began to live an aspect of the truth, emphasising this particular part of the revelation. They were blessed and hence blessed others. Later on they became engrossed in denominational issues. All that was left was the name. What happened? While the Holy Spirit found sensitivity in them he could work through them and in their area. Once the flesh wanted to contaminate the work with human programmes the Lord spoke, advised, warned and in the end since they did not pay attention he went off to work in another place. God began something new with other lives who were simple and sincere, yielding and seeking, and so it has gone on until our times. But today is decisive, He will wait no longer, there is something going on which will not be repeated again, **it is our only opportunity**.

It is regrettable that we see and hear men with no spiritual authority state what is or is not needed in the Church of the Lord. God does not need brilliant scholars or scientists who put controls on the work of the Holy Spirit. The people of God cannot go forward like that. What the church needs is lives rendered unconditionally to the direction of the Holy Spirit of God. He knows what is needed to be done, for he knows the mind of God. Thus we will see that which we desire so much.

We have to watch that other interests do not cloud our vision. God is not waiting any longer. Don't get comfortable. Don't be self-indulgent; many others have been, at a level where the slightest slip brings death. We have to stay humble. In the field of service to Christ there are no diplomas, and we have not yet attained what Jesus has called us to. May the Lord keep us away from professionalism; there is already enough wrong without adding anything else. There are already many preachers who preach themselves instead of Christ, and who preach lies and deceit. We have to be cleansed of the sin of self-sufficiency and of the division between the brothers, otherwise we will be judged guilty. Let us be clothed with the light, speaking the truth to one another, full of integrity. Let us love from the heart, without pretence. Let us not damage the Lord's inheritance. If you cannot build, **do not destroy**. Don't add to the work of the devil, for he who does not gather with Christ scatters.

Let us permit the Holy Spirit to exercise his faithful ministry. He will teach us, remind us, guide us, transform us in the faithful image of Jesus Christ the Lord, and manifest in us his power and his glory. He will use us to build up the church with spiritual wisdom and knowledge, according to God's design. Such will be the cloud of glory over the sanctuary that it will fill everything.

'Be still, and know that I am God.' We have to wait on him, for he has promised to sustain us without delay, when we have done everything that he has said.

Chapter 7

The Anointing of Kings and Priests

What is the Anointing?

Holy anointing must be differentiated from the oils which were used cosmetically as a symbol of honour, or for victory, or for burial. Jesus taught his disciples to anoint themselves in times of fasting (Matthew 6:17). Anointing was also used in times of mourning (2 Samuel 12:20). Holy Anointing is different.

There was a special preparation which God described to Moses (Exodus 30:22–33),

> 'Make these into a sacred anointing oil, a fragrant blend, the work of a perfumer. It will be the sacred anointing oil.'

Any application outside of God's purposes was prohibited. Anything it was used on was consecrated, the tabernacle and all its artifacts, everything in God's service had to be anointed.

In the previous chapter God had said that it was not just the natural abilities of the craftsmen who worked on the tabernacle that were required; they must also be filled with the Holy Spirit. The spiritual has to be understood with a spirit of wisdom and knowledge. They were capable, but in order to serve God they needed **anointing**. Note the words:

> *'Do not pour it on men's bodies and do not make any oil with the same formula.'* (Exodus 30:32)

The anointing was not to be imitated, nor was it for carnal men. The anointing is for the service of the sanctuary. The anointing speaks of service; the incense speaks of adoration. No stranger could be anointed. In order to have a part in this, a new birth is required.

The Spiritual Significance of the Anointing

The anointing is to qualify, enable, and authorise a person or thing for a specific function relating to God or to the worship of God. They anointed:

The Priests	(Exodus 28:41)
The Kings	(1 Samuel 9:16)
The Prophets	(1 Kings 19:16)

The anointing consecrates, imparting something of the holiness of God, and imparting something of his power.

It affects everything that it touches (Exodus 30:29). When a man is anointed everything he touches is also affected. Acts 19:11–12 shows how Paul, with the power of God, did extraordinary miracles. Even handkerchiefs and aprons that had touched him, when taken to the sick, had the effect of curing illness and driving out evil spirits. In Christ's Church the Holy Spirit anoints the believers, but it is a pity that so few realise the full significance of this.

> *'But you have an anointing from the Holy One, and all of you know the truth.'* (1 John 2:20)

> *'As for you, the anointing you received from him remains in you, and you do not need anyone to teach you.'* (1 John 2:27)

The oil is a symbol of the Holy Spirit. The apostles anointed the needy for their physical deliverance. James teaches the procedure when one of the community is sick:

> *'... and anoint him with oil in the name of the Lord.'* (James 5:14)

The anointing enables us to perform a function within the divine plans. Why do we not see the fullness of this anointing in the Church? There always were men with a special anointing, and today we can still see men qualified by the anointing they have received, but will they continue to be just a few? Let us see some examples that will help us to understand.

The anointing of Saul – 1 Samuel 10:1–9.

> *'"The Spirit of the LORD will come upon you in power, and you will prophesy with them; and you **will be changed into a different person."** ... As Saul turned to leave Samuel, God changed Saul's heart, and all these signs were fulfilled that day.'* (1 Samuel 10:6, 9)

Samuel had poured out the oil over Saul's head and had kissed him, the first king over the people of God had been anointed (1 Samuel 10:1–7). God had worked in this man and as a result what he did became significant. He could now do what others could not. He could go where others were afraid to go. It is a shame that Saul was not faithful to his commitment to God. Faithfulness to our covenant with the Lord is fundamental for us. But we will never be faithful in our responsibilities without first being faithful

*Faithful in being what God
wants us to be
.... to do*

Living in the Anointing

to God himself. Faithful first in being what God wants us
to be, and therefore being faithful to what God wants us
to do. This is how God goes about looking for a man who
is at one with his heart. The recommendation made to the
prophet is the same that today serves us:

> *'Do not consider his appearance or his height, for I
> have rejected him. The LORD does not look at the
> things man looks at. Man looks at the outward appear-
> ance, but the LORD looks at the heart.'*
>
> (1 Samuel 16:7)

Seven handsome men seemed to fit the conditions that
humanly were needed to be king, but God did not choose
any of them. David, who was the youngest, had not even
been taken into account. They went to fetch him from
caring for his father's sheep in the field. God said to the
prophet when David was presented to him:

> *' "Rise and anoint him; he is the one." So Samuel took
> the horn of oil and anointed him in the presence of his
> brothers, and from that day on the Spirit of the LORD
> came upon David in power.'*   (1 Samuel 16:12–13)
>
> *'I have found David my servant; with my sacred oil I
> have anointed him.'*   (Psalm 89:20)

David's relationship with God had already begun
before he was anointed. In the loneliness of the field, on
more than one occasion, he put his faith in God to the
test. *'Your servant has killed both the lion and the bear'*
(1 Samuel 17:34–37), was the testimony that he gave to
Saul. This is the record of his background; the Bible does
not contain another.

He had learned to fight in the name of Jehovah and he
knew how to save his lambs. If an animal turned on him

he would break its jawbone, and would be left with a piece of lion or bear in each hand. Surely it was not because of his muscles, just as Samson's exploits were not due to his natural strength, strong though he was. The anointing came upon them and they were invincible. In the solitude of the field, while his brothers were being prepared for war, he learned to depend on God for his defence. There he established contact and communion with the Lord. He learned to speak to God and began to receive answers from him. I imagine seeing the boy when all the people went up to celebrate their solemn assemblies. Perhaps unnoticed by the eyes of many he would take his place and there sit listening. He would be impressed by the great works of his God by the hand of those giants of faith who left their mark in history. The God of the patriarchs and prophets was the same God that he had. Why not try to reach him? Could it be possible? Would God accede to the desires of his heart? It would be a question of starting. So he started! How great were the results!

Why do you think that God chose David? God falls in love with a person who is thirsty for him, for his power, and for his purposes. We need a hunger and a thirst for the anointing that melts, penetrates, and breaks the yoke of bondage (Isaiah 10:27 KJV).

Surely David's young mind processed all these things and his vivid imagination allowed him to see so realistically the expressions of victory; images of Abraham, Isaac, Jacob, Moses, Joshua and many others,

> *'who through faith conquered kingdoms, administered justice, and gained what was promised; who shut the mouths of lions, quenched the fury of the flames, and escaped the edge of the sword; whose weakness was turned to strength; and who became powerful in battle and routed foreign armies.'* (Hebrews 11:33–34)

There were those who time and again crossed the desert, in the school of God, paying the price of the anointing that was invested in them. David reached a longing in his soul for something higher than the pleasures that all the common people chose. What others loved he threw out as rubbish to gain the excellence of the knowledge of God.

Kingship Imparted

The gap that Moses left was not easy to fill. Someone had to put their feet in the prints of the most humble man in all the world. Attested by God:

> *'Now Joshua son of Nun was filled with the spirit of wisdom because Moses had laid his hands on him. So the Israelites listened to him and did what the LORD had commanded Moses.'*   (Deuteronomy 34:9)

Moses, before he died, imparted the anointing that was in him and Joshua completed the assignment. He took the people into Canaan and divided up the promised land.

When Moses was ministering in the tabernacle Joshua stayed close, confidently affirming and trusting in the words of God. The earth shook, and fire and smoke rested on the mountain. The figure of Moses was silhouetted against the light of the glory that radiated from the presence of God. Slowly the man of God climbed. From afar Joshua looked on; some day he himself would get close to that glory. How could God not choose a man like that?

When we desire God more that anything else in the world, then truly we have found him.

Strange events surrounded the life of Elijah. God had to take him sometime, but a successor was needed to continue the task of the prophet. Elijah found the man whom God had chosen, out working in the fields, plough-ing. It was Elisha. God always chooses busy people; all of whom he called he found in their places of work. In God's business there is no room for the lazy, the irresponsible or the lethargic, those who love their own comfort. Elijah imparted the anointing on his successor just as Moses had done for his successor. He anointed Elisha son of Shaphat to succeed him as prophet (1 Kings 19:16). In this way the ministry of prophet would continue. To impart something you must have it yourself in the first place. You can use the correct words, mannerisms and prayers, but you cannot impart what you do not have. 'What we have we give you,' said Peter and John to the paralytic. We can give what we have. Whether we like it or not, conscious or unconscious, we impart what we are and what we have. For this reason it is important what we **are**.

The quality of our lives and ministries is fundamentally important! When we minister we transmit not only our virtues but also our weaknesses. God seeks out the quality in us because he is looking for a great multiplication. He does not just want a lot of poor quality, nor even a little of good quality, but a lot of good quality. If Christ has not already returned, there will be a huge inheritance of those who succeed us in the continuation of the ministry. Then we will have done good service to God.

Respecting the Anointing

We live in days when there has been almost a total lack of respect for anything. We Christians have also felt the proximity of this sweeping avalanche. Through a careless approach in both speech and action, many have been rendered ineffective because of a disrespectful attitude to the flow of the anointing. Many times I have read the notices on the electricity pylons: 'DANGER, HIGH VOLTAGE'. We ought to read the same regarding the anointing that God has placed in the men who he uses. We can all serve God, but **not all** have the same standing in the Kingdom of the Father. As far as salvation is concerned, the price paid is the same for anyone. We have all cost the same price; there is no difference one from another. But in service there are different ranks. It is not a question here of discriminating between people, but of accepting the authority (anointing) to serve. The angels differ in function and authority, whether those who serve God or those of the kingdom of darkness (Ephesians 6:12). Gifts and talents operate in the body of Christ, but gifts are to be distinguished from ministries. These ministries are anointed men, given to the body, and there is an order of authority.

> *'Do not touch my anointed ones; do my prophets no harm.'* (1 Chronicles 16:22)

He who treats the man of God disrespectfully touches the apple of his eye. In other words he puts his finger in God's eye (Zechariah 2:8). David lived for years fleeing from Saul who was hunting him down to kill him. He knew that Saul had been rejected for ever, but Saul insisted on ruling in the flesh, no longer sustained by God's Spirit. David, on the other hand, continued to grow. He was the new king over the people of God. On more than one occasion he had the life of his persecutor in his hand for the taking, but he did not want to harm him. He refused to reach out his hand to slay, through respect for the anointing that was upon the king. He had cut off a piece of Saul's robe, and even this was enough to trouble him. When the messenger brought the bad news from the battle David asked him:

> *'Why were you not afraid to lift your hand to destroy the LORD's anointed?'* (2 Samuel 1:14)

So he had him killed. David felt grief because Saul had perished like one who had not been anointed with oil (2 Samuel 1:14–27).

The words of the apostle are a serious warning.

> *'Bold and arrogant, these men are not afraid to slander celestial beings.'* (2 Peter 2:10–12; see also Jude 8–9)

How easy it is to cast aspersions and make unspiritual comments on the lives of holy people! Many people do not realise why so many things go wrong in their lives, why they are ill, why they have no desire to seek God. We all have to recognise our faults in this area. When Ananias and Sapphira lied about the price of the sale of their property Peter did not say to them: 'why did you lie to me?', no, he said 'you have lied to the Holy Spirit'. They did not know of what spirit they were. When they died for this sin great fear came upon all who heard about it.

There is no anointing for carnal men. God will not give this anointing to someone who does not respect it in the life of another. Nor will he give it to those who do not value it, nor to those who do not genuinely desire it. The self-centred, the miserly, and those with ulterior motives will not receive it. But those who are not afraid of being consumed in God's holy fire, who do not fear their own obscurity as long as God shines out, will indeed walk in the flow of the anointing. Such will be like Elisha whose bones continued to give life even after his death. David, the man who loved and longed for the Lord, received the anointing and treated it with respect, and he became great in God; as a fighter, as a poet, as a king, and as a musician. When Saul was tormented by evil spirits David played the harp, the demons left Saul and he was set free. Even when he had fallen into that terrible sin, all that David wanted was not to lose the Holy Spirit;

> *'Do not cast me from your presence or take your Holy*
> *Spirit from me.'*   (Psalm 51:11)

How could such a man not touch the heart of God?

Many who sinned wanted to be treated like David, to be accepted and forgiven as he was. But they did not want to hear those who went to reprimand them. David was not like that. Nor did they wish to lose their positions, benefits and honours. They struggled for other things, but not for the Holy Spirit, and preferred other honours before those of God. We may interpret things to suit ourselves but let us not deceive ourselves, because we cannot deceive God.

There has to be an urgent petition from us: that when we pray, preach, teach, sing and praise with musical instruments, and even in silence, we give off the aroma of the fragrance of the anointing!

Somebody said: 'the extremist lives under the law of the pendulum'. It is hard to find an attitude that is truly open and balanced. We tend to swing between overvaluing or underestimating people and things. We should give the Holy Spirit room to teach us to make judgments without fear of getting it wrong. Just as there are people who have no respect for the anointing, there are also those who confuse the ministry with the man. This is dangerous, we are not following man's ideas nor men separate from their function. We may follow a man of God, but in the Lord.

Elisha loved Elijah, respected him and served him. He was subject to a ministry. But the prophet was not the final last word for him, even though he was a man of God and the means by which God achieved his purposes. Even the best of men in the end is still a man. The sons of the prophets went to look for Elijah against the advice of Elisha. Meanwhile Elisha sought the anointing of Elijah; that is the root of the difference. Some will look for the man, others will seek the anointing.

Moses was ordered to put a veil over his face so that the sons of Israel would not set their eyes on him; for the glory of God was reflected in his countenance. We should love and respect the man and the anointing that is in him, following in the Lord. We should not overvalue, but neither should we underestimate, because if God did not forgive the pagan king who desecrated the vessels of the sanctuary and who paid with his life for his profanity and lack of respect ... how much more are we responsible if we touch the vessels that serve him who is perfection?

Character

Saul	(1 Samuel 15:1–11)
Samson	(Judges 13:25, 16:16–22)
Balaam	(Numbers 22:8–12)

These three men were used by God for a particular time and, with the exception of Samson (who is mentioned in the list of the heroes of faith in Hebrews 11:32), are not mentioned as those approved. Blind and in the last moments of his life, repentant, he asked the Lord to strengthen him once more. So Samson on the occasion of his death killed more enemies than in the whole of his life. These men were used, God had raised them up and the Spirit of God had come upon them. They were, despite themselves, used by God to some extent in achieving divine purposes. They were anointed but they were short on character. They had not been shaped. They had a lot of foliage but little root; a lot of size but not much of a foundation. A tree with a good root and not too much foliage remains firm through the storm. The firmest tree does not grow too high, using its energy to gain a good grounding.

I heard of a young man from another country who had received certain spiritual gifts and who brought about a revival for a time; what happened in his meetings was admirable. Suddenly he became involved in a series of diversions that twisted his life. Experienced brothers helped him and put him back on the right course, but no more was heard of him. I think that the latter silence was more than eloquent. No, there are no guarantees that the fruit will last. Many works were raised up which later on made a great noise as they fell. This young man needed to walk with the Lord, he had not been through God's school, nor had he been through a wilderness in his life. Time is an important factor when we go with God. Jesus was nearly three and a half years forming his disciples. Paul mentions having given again and again the same teaching, giving the whole counsel of God to his disciples over a period of three years (Acts 20:27, 31).

You cannot be a father without first being a son. We need to be conceived, formed, prepared and anointed for the work of the ministry for the building up of the body of Christ.

Kings and Priests

Jesus has made us *'kings and priests unto God and his Father'* (Revelation 1:6 KJV).

> *'No-one takes this honour upon himself; he must be called by God, just as Aaron was.'* (Hebrews 5:4)

What we are in God is affirmed in the Word. *'You **are** the salt of the earth'* (Matthew 5:13). *'You **are** the light of the world'* (Matthew 5:14). What Christ has done for us was shown a long time ago. There are people who **try** to be salt and to be light. In this way they negate Jesus' declaration. We used to spend time trying to kill off the old nature; asking God to kill the 'I'. The profound and true declaration of God is that he considers us having

already died with Christ. What do we understand from Revelation 1:6? Can you believe that Jesus has already made you a king and a priest for God? It is important to be conscious of our limitations; to know that we are but a fleeting breath that goes and does not return.

> *'Stop trusting in man, who has but a breath in his nostrils. Of what account is he?'* (Isaiah 2:22)

When we relate man to God we can say with the psalmist:

> *'what is man that you are mindful of him, the son of man that you care for him?'* (Psalm 8:4)

Just the thought is amazing and humbling. For this reason a certain amount of introspection is healthy, in the right sense of the word, so that we remain humble. We have to know that it is only by his grace and mercy that we are not consumed. But to live continually repeating what is our human weakness does not bring glory to the Lord. It is good to be broken and humbled before God, but **not** because of the circumstances. Do not underestimate yourself. If you pronounce 'I am nothing, I'm no use, I can't do anything', know that God already knows it. Jesus said: 'Without me you can do nothing.' Then we say: 'I deserve nothing, I am worthless, mere scum.' Does what we say agree with what Jesus has made us – his sons? Does it agree with what Jesus has made us for God the Father? What he made ... did he not do it well? Are we not able to believe his work in us? The apostle says:

> *'... since you have taken off your old self with its practices and have put on the new self, which is being renewed in knowledge in the image of its Creator.'*
> (Colossians 3:9–10)

We cannot belittle this amazing state of grace; what we were we are no longer. We must not dig up what God has buried. The blood of Christ satisfied God. The sacrifice of the Son of God is perfect. Let us trust in the Word of God. We are not to become light, we are not to become salt, we are not to become kings and priests; **we already are**. Christ made it so. When we understand what we are, we can begin to act accordingly. Perhaps you never behaved like a king or a priest because you thought you were a nobody. Man is the result of what he thinks.

Start today like a son of God by holding these thoughts in your mind and heart. Get rid of negative thoughts, so that you may escape evil, for you become what you think and confess. With what we confess we bind and we release,

> *'For it is with your heart that you believe and are justified, and it is with your mouth that you confess and are saved.'* (Romans 10:10)

We can illustrate this truth with an example. The Hebrew nation had many kings. Amongst them there were some who were not old enough to govern alone. They did not go out to war, nor did they take decisions on their own. They were surrounded by mature people who guided them, but when they matured things changed. But at no time did they cease to be what they were; kings. We too have been made kings and priests; we have a double anointing for a double service. How does a king behave? If we have to take the information of the scriptures we will find the best answer if we look at those who obeyed God. They governed in God's name and they were an expression of his authority. They led their men out to war and watched over their domain. This is just what we have to do in the extension and establishment of the

Kingdom of God. The kingly anointing is to extend the domain of the King of kings and Lord of lords.

The priestly anointing, on the other hand, enables us to intercede, preach and teach. When we look to God, we represent the people before God. When we look to the people, we represent God before the people. Ministering to God and to men. We should not confuse the two offices; both have their time of action.

We can see that every believer is, upon being born again, a king and priest for God, made so by Jesus Christ. As we grow and as we go on developing, mature brothers help to train us and men with a ministry edify us in order that we may take our place in the building up of the Church of the Lord.

Good is the Enemy of Best

We must not conform to less than what God wants us to be and to do. We have all that he has given us in Christ. God certainly does not want us to conform with less. He expects us to have a holy dissatisfaction with our present achievements. There is more and we should seek it, not being content to stay as we are. Many have gone cold because of staying as they were. For this reason God looks for a man amongst his own people. When he finds him he puts him through the desert to prove him, to give him a personal knowledge of God, to reveal his purposes and to show him his resources. This man must learn to live in the dimension of the Kingdom. He must move in the abundant flow of the anointing and work in accordance with God's design.

Join with me in my desire: I want all that God has, I will not be satisfied with less, **there is more**. We only have one life and not two. We will only pass through here once and never again. What we fail to do here and now we will have failed to do for the whole of eternity. On the other hand what we have done is done for ever. When we arrive on the other side there will not be time to return, reform or recant. It is now or never. Shall we be able to look on him when he comes and not be ashamed?

The Ten Virgins

This story is well known, and is for us a good illustration and example. The ten virgins had lamps and the ten lamps were shining, all ten were waiting for the bride-groom, all ten became drowsy as they waited in the night vigil; but only at the moment of action was the difference discovered. Five of them had reserve jars of oil. The other five were distressed to see that their oil was not sufficient and there was no time to make provision. They asked the others to provide the precious fluid so that they would not lose their right of entry to the wedding. The tragic reply was, *'go to those who sell oil and buy some for yourselves.'* They had lost their opportunity (Matthew 25:1–13).

The word 'buy' speaks to us of paying a price. Yes, there is oil, there is abundant provision for the time of action; but we must buy, paying **the price of the anointing**.

> *'. . . how God anointed Jesus of Nazareth with the Holy Spirit and power, and how he went around doing good and healing all who were under the power of the devil, because God was with him.'* (Acts 10:38)

> *'The Spirit of the Sovereign LORD is on me, because the LORD has anointed me to preach good news to the poor.*
> *He has sent me to bind up the broken-hearted, to proclaim freedom for the captives and release from*

darkness for the prisoners, to proclaim the year of the LORD's favour and the day of vengeance of our God, to comfort all who mourn.'   (Isaiah 61:1–2)

Chapter 8

Time and Opportunity

'Therefore I tell you that the kingdom of God will be taken away from you and given to a people who will produce its fruit.' (Matthew 21:43)

It is evident that on all fronts we are going through difficult times. Just to consider the disastrous predictions from economists, scientists and futurists is terrifying. A strong and adverse current is moving in the spiritual world. All in all we have to recognise that for the church these are historic times. This is our great opportunity.

'I have seen something else under the sun: The race is not to the swift or the battle to the strong, nor does food come to the wise or wealth to the brilliant or favour to the learned; but time and chance (opportunity) *happen to them all.'* (Ecclesiastes 9:11)

'Whatever your hand finds to do, do it with all your might, for in the grave, where you are going, there is neither working nor planning nor knowledge nor wisdom.' (Ecclesiastes 9:10)

God has given us the time and the opportunity to fulfil the role that corresponds to us in this present phase. We must act now before the Kingdom is given to others.

> *'He changes times and seasons; he sets up kings and deposes them. He gives wisdom to the wise and knowledge to the discerning.'*
> (Daniel 2:21)

Every child of God has a part to play in this enterprise; but if they do not act then that part will be given to another, because God's purposes may be hindered but not impeded. God will certainly do what he has intended. We must not let this time go by, for that would be an irremedial loss. Today is the day, this is the hour. God wants to do it, so let us get on with it and make an impression.

Lost Opportunity

We cannot say that we lack opportunity. We cannot say that we do not have time. He has appointed us as kings to retain the kingdom, so that when God moves on from this time and occasion we will have done what we had to do.

Saul had not obeyed. God does not play around.

> *'"You acted foolishly," Samuel said. "You have not kept the command the LORD your God gave you; if you had, he would have established your kingdom over Israel for all time."'*
> (1 Samuel 13:13)

Jesus, the Christ, according to the flesh would have descended from Saul if the latter had obeyed. Saul lost such a great and unique opportunity. The **Lord** had torn the kingdom of Israel from him and given it to one better than he. God had rejected him and he who is the Glory of Israel does not lie or change his mind (1 Samuel 15:28–29). How his destiny had changed! God had made him a straight road but Saul tried to twist it. He considered the word of God beneath him and squandered his opportunity. David then had the privilege of gaining an eternal kingdom: the unbreakable sceptre of the Son of God.

Some people's ambitions cause them to lose their direction. Naaman had received a miracle and wanted to present gifts to the prophet of God. Elisha refused to receive anything from him so the man began to return to his homeland. Elisha's servant Gehazi went out and caught up with the officer and his retinue on the road. He lied to him in order to receive gifts, and later also lied to the man of God. Therefore he became leprous in the place of Naaman (2 Kings 5:24–27). He too scorned the great opportunity that God had given him. How different he was from his teacher!

When Elijah came by where Elisha was ploughing he came to him and laid his mantle on him, and from then on this peasant lived with just one idea; to receive the anointing of his master. When God snatched up his servant in the whirlwind Elisha was left with that mantle and the power with it. For some time before this the people had been foretelling the departure of Elijah. Even he, as time went by, made his own comments. One mistake and the great moment would have already passed by. 'Stay here, Elisha', were Elijah's words. But Elisha said, *'As surely as the LORD lives and as you live, I will not leave you.'* He repeatedly asked him to stay back but Elisha resisted. How would he manage to sleep and watch at the same time? I think that Elisha took all the precautions, so that awake or asleep, if God snatched away his master, he would know. When the man of God saw that Elisha would not leave, he made the offer which his disciple so desired.

> ' "Tell me, what can I do for you before I am taken from you?"
>
> "Let me inherit a double portion of your spirit," Elisha replied.

> *"You have asked a difficult thing," Elijah said, "yet if you see me when I am taken from you, it will be yours – otherwise not." '*   (2 Kings 2:9–10)

Such was his desire, his ambition and his passion that he took hold of his own clothes and tore them apart when the prophet was taken up. Elisha had been walking alongside his master. Why did he not ask for anything else? There are so many things that men have ambition for. Why did he not think of his personal prosperity, riches or comfort? To him these seemed small and temporal compared with his precious and coveted anointing. That is why it turned out as it did. He picked up the cloak that had fallen from Elijah and the miracles began. Elisha now had an anointing that transcended all expectation. Gehazi, however, aspired to the mantle from Naaman, the leper. What benefit did the riches of this world bring him? Now he was unclean. Sometimes I have imagined this man's condition. White from leprosy, his flesh eaten away by the terrible disease, outside the community, seated on a rock with his head between his hands, weeping. Why did he not aspire to the mantle that had belonged to Elijah and now to his master? Because his heart was on other things. Where our treasure is, there will our hearts be also.

Where is your treasure? What is your treasure? Saul wept, perhaps Gehazi too, but there was nothing else to be done, they had wasted their time and missed their opportunity. Esau also despised the blessing and the opportunity that God had given (Genesis 25:30–34).

> ' *"Look, I am about to die," Esau said. "What good is the birthright to me?" '*   (Genesis 25:32)

That is why God rejected him.

> *'Just as it is written: "Jacob I loved, but Esau I hated."'*
> (Romans 9:13)

The Rights of the Firstborn

These rights were something spiritual that required faith to possess. They received:

(a)   The rights of priesthood.
(b)   The parental line of the Saviour.
(c)   Rights and privileges.
(d)   Double inheritance.
(e)   Authority.

If Esau had taken advantage of such a great opportunity, the order would have been different. Abel – Seth – Shem – Abraham – Esau. But it was not like that. In his place the name of his brother Jacob appears. Hebrews 12:17 says that

> *'He could bring about no change of mind, though he sought the blessing with tears.'*

Genesis tells how desperate he was when his father declared *'Your brother ... took your blessing.'* Jacob was the younger and knew well what the firstborn rights meant. Esau sold it for a plate of stew. Some value to place on such a great matter! Jacob lied to his father and he ran away, he was insolent and also a coward. Nevertheless God says: *'Jacob I loved.'* He put him through his schooling and made him a father of multitudes. The last subject matter of this chapter is when he wrestled with the angel. Jacob said

> *'I will not let you go unless you bless me.'*
> (Genesis 32:26)

Even in the struggle he esteemed the blessing of God as of
prime value over all else.

Holy Ambition

'Daniel, a man greatly beloved.'

(Daniel 10:11–12 AV)

For many years during his captivity Daniel occupied the
highest positions in the empire. Kings and governors
changed, but he continued in his place of honour. He
enjoyed great privileges. Why bother to pray three times
a day? Why grieve? Why fast? Did he not have power,
riches and honour? But these things did not satisfy him.
His satisfaction was in the realisation of the purposes of
God for his people. This desire consumed him; his passion
was for God himself. His thoughts were God's thoughts;
his desires were God's desires. He insisted and persisted
until his nation returned out of captivity. What a challenge is the life of Daniel!

God wants to know up to what point are we prepared
to persist for his blessing.

Jesus used a parable to teach on this matter. Always
pray and do not give up (Luke 18:1–8). There was a
widow who kept coming to the unjust judge who neither
feared God nor cared about men. The story tells us that
she did not give up when the weather was cold or hot or
when it rained. It says that by bothering him she wore
down his resistance and he had to eventually give her
justice. We are not prevailing upon a judge like that. Our
God is just, faithful and true. He urges us to ask, seek and
knock; giving us the assurance that everyone who asks
receives; he who seeks finds; and to him who knocks, the
door will be opened (Matthew 7:7–11).

God is not inconvenienced by those who seek him at an
inopportune time. In a certain house at around midnight

someone is knocking at the door asking for three loaves; a friend has arrived and he has nothing to set before him. The neighbour replies,

> *'Don't bother me. The door is already locked, and my children are with me in bed. I can't get up and give you anything.'* (Luke 11:7)

But because of his insistence he got what he wanted.

Ask, seek and cry out, with agony in your soul, like Hannah did (1 Samuel 1:7–20). For a woman in those times it was a disgrace to be barren. For us too it is a disgrace to be barren and without fruit. We have to cry out until God takes away our disgrace. Let us not lose the opportunity that he, our Lord, gives to us.

Let us use the time of our brief pilgrimage. Every second, every minute, every hour, every day, every week, every month and every year that goes by without profit for eternity, will never be available to us again. Let us ask, call and seek the Lord until our last breath, until our last heartbeat, living for God and for his cause.

There is to be released upon men and women an anointing so great that they will not be able to resist. May we be amongst the courageous men of Gideon who 'lapped the water' (Judges 7). May God not pass us by. In the days when Jesus was born, the angels bypassed the powerful organisations and the religious bodies and went instead to humble shepherds. The same happened when the Lord began his ministry; he did not go to the synagogues to find his disciples.

History is repeated. God has removed people from the temples on more than one occasion in the course of time. Those who appear to be something are really nothing. God is restoring man and he is restoring families. With these families he is establishing a people. He is taking from them things previously regarded as essential or of prime importance, but which are really of no consequence.

I know people who spend many hours on their knees, people who fast over extended periods, groaning with tears for an awakening, for a greater anointing in these glorious and decisive days. This is the army of God! Don't lose this time and opportunity! This is the time! This is God's hour in the clock of eternity. His great signs for planet earth are taking place.

We should not be spectators; there is no room for us on the balcony. We are the actors, the lead characters, the protagonists. *The scene is beginning, the curtain is rising! ... and the Son of God is returning in the clouds of heaven with power and great glory.*

Chapter 9

The Great Work

God was ready to liberate Israel by the hand of Gideon. This man had been given the word by the angel and the signs had been confirmed. Nevertheless God had to give him one more confirmation. On approaching the enemy camp he was able to overhear a conversation. Gideon arrived just as a man was telling a friend his dream.

> *'"I had a dream," he was saying. "A round loaf of barley bread came tumbling into the Midianite camp. It struck the tent with such force that the tent over-turned and collapsed."'* (Judges 7:13)

The Church is the body of Christ.

> *'For we, though many, are one bread and one body; for we all partake of that one bread.'*
> (1 Corinthians 10:17 NKJV)

This is the declaration. Whether we like it or not we are one bread and we are one single body.

When I think of a loaf of bread, I think of one made from wheat. I think of the **long process** that the grain from different ears has to go through, until it becomes bread. After **harvest** it is **winnowed**, **cleaned**, and then **milled**. It is

crushed and **ground** until the **individual grains are no longer identifiable**. The process has been such that it has been transformed into white flour. After that it is **kneaded** into dough. **Water** and **salt** give it **shape**, and then it goes into the oven; the **fire** finishes the process.

I believe that this is what the Lord is doing with the church. The grains of wheat made into bread speak of unity. It was from the summit of the mountain that a **loaf of bread** began to roll. This is the picture of the Church on the move; and it will wreak havoc in the enemy camp. We Christians are in a process, being tested, brought into unity, and perfected in love. The tumbling loaf of bread is the movement of the Church on the advance.

The instructions given through Gideon are also significant. The clay jars had to be empty, with a torch burning inside each jar. How many times has God not been able to put in the fire of the Spirit because lives have been found to be full up with other things. Resolute, breaking the jars, sounding the trumpets and shouting in the name of God and of their leader. Broken lives proclaiming the message of God with the sound of voice and trumpet. Empty of self and of other things, but full of holy fire, which is the ingredient that takes hold of the great victory.

> *'I have commanded my holy ones; I have summoned my warriors to carry out my wrath – those who rejoice in my triumph. Listen, a noise on the mountains, like that of a great multitude! Listen, an uproar among the kingdoms, like nations massing together! The LORD Almighty is mustering an army for war.'*
>
> (Isaiah 13:3–4)

God is mustering his great and powerful army. Watch! This is for the consecrated and the courageous, for those who rejoice in the glory of God. Jesus said:

> *'From the days of John the Baptist until now, the kingdom of heaven has been forcefully advancing, and forceful men lay hold of it.'* (Matthew 11:12)

It needs strength and courage to take hold of the kingdom. It is not a matter of taking something easily given, but aggressively seizing it by force and with power. There is no other way but to face up to the task with realism and with passion, with deliverance and with transformed lives. Seek first his kingdom and his righteousness, and ***all*** these things will be given to you as well (Matthew 6:33).

Others have sown with tears. We harvest what others have sown and then watered with prayer. Thousands have passed on to eternity without seeing even a part of what they so much desired for God. We continue this work which is not yet finished, the ***reaping is to come***.

> *'He who wins souls is wise.'* (Proverbs 11:30)

> *'All hard work brings a profit, but mere talk leads only to poverty.'* (Proverbs 14:23)

It's time for action, not for passing the time looking skywards like astronomers. Let us fear God, love him and serve him. God has made us more than victorious.

> *'But thanks be to God, who always leads us in triumphal procession in Christ.'* (2 Corinthians 2:14)

> *'In all these things we are more than conquerors through him who loved us.'* (Romans 8:37)

We can live in the power of the resurrection of Christ, breaking out of mediocrity. God has already given us all we need.

The Two Pools

There was a pool in Jerusalem which was surrounded by five covered colonnades, where a great number of disabled people used to lie, waiting for healing through the waters. The blind, the lame, and the paralysed waited, because from time to time an angel came down to the pool and stirred the water, and the first one who got in after the movement of the water was cured of any ailment.

> *'One who was there had been an invalid for thirty-eight years. When Jesus saw him lying there and learned that he had been in this condition for a long time, he asked him, "Do you want to get well?" "Sir," the invalid replied, "I have no-one to help me into the pool when the water is stirred. While I am trying to get in, some-one else goes down ahead of me." '* (John 5:5–7)

The pool was called Bethesda which means 'House of mercy'. We could therefore call that pool 'the pool of the house of mercy'.

There are congregations like that pool – stagnant. There is no flow of life. Things do not always happen there, and when something does it is simply by mercy. From time to time they may receive a small experience. Perhaps some angel of God comes along who preaches with anointing and ministers deliverance, then the water is stirred and a few are touched by the power of God. All around this church community there are multitudes of stricken people lying around. These needy people are so near to the congregation, but nobody gets them into the church, except when an angel comes. Maybe one of them could reach the place by themselves, but they arrived too late; and in just a short while everything has returned to what it was like before – stagnant. Thousands die just a little each day, but they have nobody who will put them in contact with Christ.

But there was another pool in Jerusalem, the pool of Siloam. Note that these two pools mentioned were in the same city, but different things happened in them. This is what happens in different communities belonging to the church; some are stagnant, others in contrast grow and grow both numerically and spiritually.

What a sad picture is presented by the pool of Bethesda! But the pool of Siloam was not like that. The interpretation of Siloam is 'Sent'. The dictionary says: 'One who sends or gives direction'. Jesus sent the man who had been blind from birth to wash his eyes in this pool (John 9:6–14). So the man went and washed, and came home seeing.

The pool of Siloam had this name because the water that reached it came from another place. Its source was a spring. On the outskirts of Jerusalem there was a fountain called Gihon, and this spring was connected to the pool of Siloam. King Hezekiah had a tunnel dug for a conduit to connect the spring to the pool. Before this excavation the connection was made by an aqueduct that was designed in such a way as to present a serious disadvantage in times of war, because the enemies could enter the city via the aqueduct and over the wall. It was necessary to cut right through a hill, and so an underground connection was made (2 Kings 20:20; 2 Chronicles 32:30).

Our lives have to be connected to the source of the water that will become a spring welling up to eternal life. Jesus speaks of this. Those who receive him are transformed into a fountain of living water, moreover rivers of living water will flow within. This is marvellous, wonderful communion, abundant life, a glorious life. However, a superficial connection is a danger in the daily war that we face against the flesh and against the devil. When communion with the Lord is superficial, the enemy can enter and from there destroy. Everything has its price. We have to go deep, it requires effort to penetrate the heart of the mountain, in order to gather the water of life, the water that purifies, and so avoid the danger of enemy interference. Be united to the Lord to be strong through his mighty strength; this is the only way the enemy cannot enter.

Returning to the pool, no angel came to stir the water at Siloam; it was always moving. There were no needy people there surrounding the pool. Jesus sent the blind man there to remove the mud from his eyes so that he could see. Many sons of God are like this. Jesus can send the blind and needy to them and they will make them see. They have life and they have power because they are well connected to Jesus. What the Lord did, so can they do, bearing fruit that will last. This is the people that God is preparing. They will overflow the limits of the imagination! Get ready! Don't stay on the outside!

Both the paralytic and the blind man, at the two pools, were both healed on the Sabbath day of rest. For the religious people it was more important not to break the rules than to see a miracle by the same God who ordered rest and who made the day for it. That is how it was, and today it is still the same. The foolish Pharisees could say:

> 'It is the Sabbath; the law forbids you to carry your mat.'   (John 5:10)

But they were unable to release him from his bonds. Many today are an open Bible, but only that! They can show what should not be done, but cannot give what others need to receive. Is it not glorious that on a day consecrated to God miracles should occur? But if it had been within their power to prevent these miracles they would have surely done so. It does not matter if the blind man cannot see; let him see the Sabbath or not see at all!

These people are like some Christians who criticise their brothers for the way they minister, but they themselves cannot do it better or even the same. They are perfectionists, but they ***don't do anything***. They should rejoice when God is using somebody because he who is not against him is for him.

We must leave behind our conventions and our techniques which look so good but which do not yield results. We have to seek a union with the Lord that is not so superficial. It has to be deep, so that the church is prepared for the greatest birthing of its history, and the Christians who are not in on it will get left behind or outside. The labour pains are already beginning; it is not a game. This is getting serious, friend, and it is going to be tremendous. Saint Paul did not find a better example to express his spiritual situation to his beloved and stubborn disciples:

> *'My dear children, for whom I am again in the pains of childbirth until Christ is formed in you...'*
>
> (Galatians 4:19)

The gravity of the situation means that the future mother has to deny herself of many things for the love of the son which is to be born.

I have been at a delivery. The life of one person is put at risk against the life of the one who is to be brought into the world. The exertion is such that one or other can die, and the lack of proper effort and attention may result in injury, or at the very least some considerable discomfort. A hard couch, pain, groans, blood and tears, the future mother greatly moved and disturbed, until at last..., the new life. The baby has only just been born and she wants to know how it is and what it is. Only then can the mother rest and sleep, the trace of a triumphant smile on her suffering face.

This is what Paul was saying. I am again in the pains of childbirth until Christ is formed in you, until you are made in the image of Jesus Christ. Are we aware of the significance of the Great Harvest? The Holy Spirit who helps us, produces in us character and strength. With such qualities we may take up the role which we are expected to fulfil as sons of God in this decisive hour of God's dealings with the human race.

> *'May the LORD, the God of your fathers, increase you a thousand times and bless you as he has promised!'*
> (Deuteronomy 1:11)

The H.S. Help us

Produces in us Character
+ Strength

With such Qualities we may
take up the Role which we
are expected to fulfil as
sons of God

Chapter 10

Our Own Steps in the Vision

Each one of us at one time or another has suffered humiliation as a result of our own acts of arrogant behaviour. God brings down the proud and keeps them afar off; the Lord raises up the humble of heart and resists the haughty. We do not have, humanly speaking, anything to be proud of. Moreover, we must not be proud. Instead we follow the One who was obedient to death on the cross, who though being in very nature God, made himself nothing, so that we in his poverty might become enriched. Since all we have received is from the Lord, and nothing is our own, even our lives do not belong to us. Jesus is our great and excellent Lord, so our constant attitude has to be that of one crucified on the cross of Christ. The new nature is what must be seen in us, and for this we should view ourselves from God's perspective. That is to say, how God sees us.

The old should not be mixed with the new. We have been regenerated by God to the new life, we have nothing to do with our old life. There are people who live remembering what was before. They were baptised, burying the old life, but they stay weeping over the grave. They carry on looking at themselves from the perspective of the flesh. They feel continually in debt, even though Jesus already paid everything to God on their behalf. They are more aware of their own limitations than of the abundant provision that God has made available in Christ. For this reason they believe that they are a nobody and do not deserve anything, continually confessing that they are nothing and are no good for anything. On the other hand they say that they rejoice in their great salvation and the victory of Jesus in their lives. A person who has been washed by the blood of Jesus, who has been forgiven and released from sin, who has been translated by God into the kingdom of light, who has received the Holy Spirit, is no longer a nothing or a nobody. The Holy Scriptures say that to those who believed he gave power to become the sons of God.

Continual confession of the negative makes human smallness appear more important than the work that Jesus did on our behalf. This sort of confession throughout life is not a symptom of humility. Acknowledging that we are sons of God through Jesus Christ is to confess the work of Jesus, which was completed to perfection, satisfying the just requirements of God. If we say that we are kings and priests for God through Jesus Christ we are not lying, although we are still only at the beginning of the process. Exalting the work of Jesus in our life is not pride, but this gives glory to his name. We are kings, but having little idea of what we are makes us live like commoners. We are like the brother of the prodigal son, the one who stayed at home. Aware of his duties and obligations, like just another labourer, he never took a lamb to have a party with his friends. Having no idea of his position resulted in never taking hold of it. That is how we live when we doubt the perfect work of Jesus.

Let us act with boldness, not doubting nor allowing others to make us doubt what we are now in Jesus. Sometimes we do tend to doubt our calling. The children of Israel grumbled and doubted regarding the man whom God had chosen for the ministry (Numbers 17:1–10).

Man should be aware of these attacks, and remember it is God who comes out in his defence. God ordered them to take twelve staffs, one from the leader of each of their ancestral tribes. They were placed before the Lord in the Tent of Meeting overnight until the next day. Each staff had inscribed on it the respective owner's name. The sign to be given was something quite incredible, indeed miraculous; the staff belonging to the man chosen was to sprout. The following morning plainly revealed which staff had the demonstration of the power of God, and now there could be no more doubts. Who could deny the testimony of God himself? Aaron's staff had not only sprouted but had budded, blossomed and produced almonds.

This is how God will bear testimony on behalf of those whom he has called. In their life they will have to wait through the dark night, anticipating the activity of the mysterious divine power, until the first light of the new dawn breaks through. There is no better testimony than that which God gives of us.

With this in mind, let us step out in the work which God has given us for the building up of the church in our area and our nation. The promise to the Hebrew nation resounded: 'Every place where you set your foot will be yours.' The promised land had already been given to them, but because it was occupied they had to fight in order to enter in. The marching order had already been given. They were not to look at the cities with walls that reached the sky, nor the giants who were the sons of Anak, nor the enemy armies with their weaponry, nor the greater strength of those forces in relation to the fighters of Israel. No, they had to go, just go and take it, no more than that. Even though it was occupied and its inhabitants not prepared to give it up without a fight, when the soles of their feet touched the place the ownership of the property had already been signed over to them. The war that the sons of Israel had to wage to enter into Canaan was not to obtain the land; for God had given it to them and it was already theirs. When they fought they were now defending their own property. The victory for this people was already assured; they fought knowing that in the end they would have success. It was like reading the beginning and the ending of a book. When later it had to be read through in its entirety they knew how it would finish, even though half way through things would take a few turns for the worse. It could not finish any other way. They had to move on the basis of God's words and the rest was already done.

God has also given to us more than victory. The Christian who struggles to achieve the victory has lost even before starting. We do not fight to win victory; we are already victorious. We do, however, struggle to retain our rights, to keep hold of the victory which Jesus gained on our behalf. In the same way when we embark on our work for God we take up a position and take possession, knowing that however much we have to fight, the victory will finally be in our hands. God subjected everything under the feet of Christ, and we as the Church of Christ are this body, we are these feet. All that we have to do is to walk in obedience to his word and he will soon crush the enemy under our feet.

No Excuses

We have always wanted to explain our failures with a 'because', wanting to justify the things which did not turn out right. How many unnecessary arguments we make to cover up our limitations! We have belittled God in our minds and in our lives, limiting the Lord in his work in us and through us. The nature of God cannot be diminished, but when we do not believe properly he is restricted and limited. He will act according to our faith. We say we could do nothing in that particular situation 'because' the people there are so hard, though in truth it was because of our indifference to the people. This is how we acknowledge that God has power for some things, but consider that he cannot reach certain people. A friend reminds us that we are the hard ones, and this is the plain truth. **Because** we did not have enough money, because it rained, **because** nobody knew us, **because** the people would not understand..., this is how we explain the failure of our work. The problem is directed at the people, the time, the scarce resources, the lack of helpers and indifference, but the problem is within ourselves.

When God's time for a place comes, when the man of God is in this place, the excuses melt away. Nobody can make God deviate, there are no people too hard, no disease that can resist, no demon that will not come out; there are no limits to the working of the power of God. Everything is possible for God and for him who believes. The obstacle is not in the people, nor in the demons, nor in the diseases, nor in the religion, nor in the lack of resources, nor even in the climate. No, we ourselves are the obstacle ... May God open our eyes! God has said this to us and the experience of the task has proved it. We are witnesses of the work of God here in the town of Goya, Argentina. Hundreds of families have been transformed into a new life. The deaf, the blind, the maimed, the mentally ill, the demonised, those with cancer and tuberculosis have all been healed by the hundred, and released from their bondage. Miracles began to occur in our ministry which the Lord gave to us to give to the people. Some people who had already passed away for several hours were even returned to life by the power of God. God responds to the simple faith of those who believe in nothing other than him and his word.

A powerful flow moves men of faith and the inexplicable happens. Let us walk with humility before our God, conscious of our position in Christ. Everything is ours, because it has all been given to Jesus Christ our Lord, and through our being united to him it is available to us who believe, love and serve him.

New Anointing

There is a new team working here in the north of Argentina for the extension of the kingdom of God. This team was birthed by God and then born in our own hearts and minds. We are learning to get mobilised into prompt action in a contemporary fashion. We have sought to prevent the work from revolving around one man, recognising that it should revolve around God. In this cause there is nobody indispensable. It functions with us, or in spite of us, and at the last resort without us, but it does go forward; its progress is not hindered. Our responsibility as God's children is great, the task that we are undertaking has to be consistent, continuing with or without us. This is the success of the ministry. We know after all that God raises up his men and anoints them to lead others and confirm their ministries. The people await, not a new religion, nor a new religious sect, not human words, nor new methods, but they wait for men and women of God who will speak the word of God with a ministry of fire. The kingdom of God does not consist of words but of power, with a demonstration of power in the Holy Spirit. We are the hope of God; where we the Church go, Christ goes too, and if we refuse to speak, then the very stones will cry out. Such is our responsibility.

It is well worth the discipline and training so that we might successfully discharge our function and ministry. Thousands of people systematically fast each day of the week, and in this way cover all the days of the year praying and fasting, ministering directly and in detail on behalf of nations and peoples, for men and women of

God in their own nation and abroad, for an awakening in all the nations, for a revival amongst the Christians, for a Great Harvest of souls. In this way, together with the work of many Christians who are aware of their responsibility, the enterprise that God has committed to us functions and goes on. We go on taking steps towards maturity, towards greater things, aiming at 'God's best', using all the means provided by God to go forward into the breach with the message that transforms lives.

Perhaps you have taken steps that were once leading you towards possession of the conquests already made by Christ, but for some time now you have only seen closed doors along your way; pressures from outside and inside have caused you to retreat, to detach and isolate you. But if on reading these simple reflections, which spring from a spirit of loyalty to God, to you and to the work of Christ, a disquiet has been stirred in you for a deeper life and for a more effective ministry, permit me to say that **if you believe, everything is possible for God**. Your life of prayer, your life of fasting, your devotion to the Holy Scriptures, can be increased to reach levels which until now you would not have imagined. If after reading with an open and sincere spirit what I have shared, you feel a holy discontent within you, then we have achieved the assignment. **I am praying for you**. Press on, God is awaiting you with new experiences in his service, fresh **anointing** will come upon your head and will pass on to those who are around you. You can receive the gifts of the Holy Spirit and develop them, you can grow in your faith and exercise a ministry that will bring devastation to the ranks of the enemy. God has not changed, he is the same Yesterday and Today and for Ever (Hebrews 13:8).

> *'Surely the arm of the LORD is not too short to save, nor his ear too dull to hear.'* (Isaiah 59:1)

God has not diminished, he does not wear out, he remains immutable forever. God is waiting for you to keep the appointment. He wants to meet with you and to lead you on, taking **steps in the dimension of his power**. Where is the God of those men of faith who went before us? He is seeking men of faith who will call on him, who will dare to trust in him; who will resist Satan, defy sin and deny the flesh, and release the power of God upon those who suffer.

Epilogue

If you wish to be upheld in a specific need for prayer and fasting by God's people, or if you have other concerns in your ministry, write to:

    Juan José Churruarín – **New Anointing**
    Casilla de Correo No. 25
    3450 – Goya
    Corrientes
    Argentina
    South America

If you have enjoyed this book and would like to help us to send a copy of it and many other titles to needy pastors in the **Third World**, please write for further information or send your gift to:

**Sovereign World Trust
PO Box 777, Tonbridge
Kent TN11 0ZS
United Kingdom**

or to the **'Sovereign World'** distributor in your country.

Visit our website at **www.sovereign-world.org** for a full range of Sovereign World books.